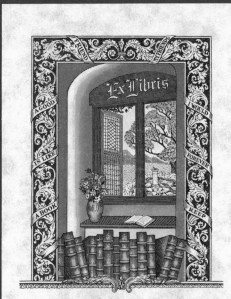

Ex Libris

Merlin H. Forster

TWAYNE'S WORLD AUTHORS SERIES

A Survey of the World's Literature

Sylvia E. Bowman, Indiana University
GENERAL EDITOR

MEXICO

John P. Dyson, Indiana University
EDITOR

Xavier Villaurrutia

(TWAS 159)

TWAYNE'S WORLD AUTHORS SERIES (TWAS)

The purpose of TWAS is to survey the major writers—novelists, dramatists, historians, poets, philosophers, and critics—of the nations of the world. Among the national literatures covered are those of Australia, Canada, China, Eastern Europe, France, Germany, Greece, India, Italy, Japan, Latin America, New Zealand, Poland, Russia, Scandinavia, Spain, and the African nations, as well as Hebrew, Yiddish, and Latin Classical literatures. This survey is complemented by Twayne's United States Authors Series and English Authors Series.

The intent of each volume in these series is to present a critical analytical study of the works of the writer; to include biographical and historical material that may be necessary for understanding, appreciation, and critical appraisal of the writer; and to present all material in clear, concise English—but not to vitiate the scholarly content of the work by doing so.

Xavier Villaurrutia

By FRANK DAUSTER

Rutgers University

Twayne Publishers, Inc.   ::   New York

For Helen

. . . only something in me understands
the voice of your eyes is deeper than all roses.

Preface

The purpose of this volume is to make available for the English-reading public a general study of the work of the Mexican poet and dramatist, Xavier Villaurrutia. In order to demonstrate the progression of his work from the early efforts to the mature production, a chronological approach seemed best, so that each of the major chapters treats the individual works in their order of composition. Although the primary concern is with the works themselves, it seemed necessary to give a relatively detailed account of the background and of the rather special circumstances surrounding Villaurrutia's association with other writers, notably the group known as the "Contemporáneos."

All of Villaurrutia's published verse and plays are considered here; the edition used is that of the *Obras*, a second edition prepared by Miguel Capistrán, Alí Chumacero, and Luis Mario Schneider. For reasons of space, and because it seemed more feasible to treat only the creative works in this initial study in English, the considerable body of Villaurrutia's criticism has not been studied except insofar as it illuminates his own work and creative theory. The bibliography employs this same criterion, including only the plays, poems, and related materials. All translations are by the author except where otherwise indicated.

I wish to thank all those who have been of assistance in the preparation of this study, including the many Mexican friends who have given generously of their time. Special thanks must go to Jane Snaidas and to my wife Helen for the help which they gave so unstintingly.

Contents

Chronology

1903   March 27. Born in Mexico City, son of Rafael Villaurrutia, a commissions agent, and Julia González de Villaurrutia, a native of Chihuahua. Although Villaurrutia's name appears in the birth records as Javier Villaurrutia y González, he apparently changed the spelling of his first name and dropped his second name at an early age.

1919   First poems published in literary reviews.

1922   With Jaime Torres Bodet and Bernardo Ortiz de Montellano, founded *La Falange*. At about this time abandoned formal study, and began to collaborate in various magazines, writing film reviews and, under the pseudonym "Microscopic Ball," reviews of bullfights. Francis Jammes' *Almaida de Etremont. Manzana de Anís* published by Cvltvra in Novo's translation with Villaurrutia's prologue.

1923   Publication by Porrúa of the anthology *Ocho poetas*, including Villaurrutia's first work in book form.

1924   *La poesía de los jóvenes de México* published by Antena.

1926   Publication of *Reflejos* by Cvltvra.

1927   Foundation of *Ulises* by Novo and Villaurrutia.

1928   A position in the Ministry of Education leads to closer relationships with other young writers and the opportunity to establish with them the journal *Contemporáneos*. *Dama de corazones* published by Edics. Ulises. Foundation with Novo of Teatro Ulises. Publication of the "Contemporáneos" joint anthology of modern Mexican poetry, culminating in critical and public furore against them.

1929   Publication of the translation of Blake's *Marriage of Heaven and Hell*.

1931   Publication by Barandal of *Dos nocturnos* and by Fábula of *Nocturnos*. Publication of the translation with Antonieta

Rivas of Gide's *La escuela de las mujeres* and Villaurrutia's edition of the *Sonetos* of Sor Juana, both by Edics. de la Razón.

1932 Foundation with Celestino Gorostiza and others of Teatro Orientación.

1933 Performance of *Parece mentira* by Orientación.

1934 Performance of *¿En qué piensas?* by Orientación. Prologue to Elías Nandino's *Eco*, published by Mundial.

1935 Edition of López Velarde's *Poemas escogidos,* published by Cvltvra. Study at Yale Drama School 1935-36 on a grant from the Rockefeller Foundation, Villaurrutia's only trip outside Mexico.

1936 Founded Drama Group of Electricians' Union, which he directed until 1939. *Nocturno de los Angeles* published by Hipocampo.

1937 *Nocturno mar* published by Hipocampo. *La pintura mexicana moderna* published in Barcelona.

1938 *Nostalgia de la muerte* published by Sur, Buenos Aires. *Ha llegado el momento* performed in the Teatro Rex. Publication by Cuadernos de México Nuevo of the never performed *Sea usted breve.*

1939 Edition of the *Poemas escogidos* of Efrén Rebolledo, published by Cvltvra. Performance of the opera *La mulata de Córdoba* in the Palacio de Bellas Artes.

1940 *Textos y pretextos* published by La Casa de España en México. Edition of Sor Juana's *Endechas* published by Taller. Prologues to Ricardo de Alcázar's translation of Valéry's *Aforismos. Discurso a los cirujanos,* published by Nueva Cvltvra, and Eduardo García Maynez' translation of Rilke's *Melodía del amor y muerte del corneta Cristóbal Rilke,* published by Letras de México. Translation and prologue to Paul Morand's *Viaje a México,* and Pirandello's *La vida que te di* (with Agustín Lazo), both published by Nueva Cvltvra.

1941 *Décima muerte* published by Nueva Voz. Publication by Séneca of *Laurel,* prepared by Villaurrutia, Paz, Gil-Albert, and Prados.

1942 Performance of *La hiedra* in the Teatro Fábregas, and *La mujer legítima* in the Teatro Ideal. The latter won second prize in a national drama contest, provoking a polemic about commercial and experimental drama. Prologue to Agustín Lazo's translation of Nerval's *Aurelia,* published by Nueva Cvltvra. Translation of Gide's *El regreso del hijo pródigo* published by Séneca. Edition of *El león y la virgen,* a selection of López Velarde's poetry, published by the Imprenta Universitaria.

1943 Publication by Letras de México of the *Autos profanos.* Villaurrutia active in the drama group Teatro de México and founds, with Octavio Barreda, the review *El hijo pródigo.*

1944 Performance of *El yerro candente* in the Teatro Fábregas. Publication by Costa-Amic of Lazo and Villaurrutia's translation of Giraudoux's *Judith.*

1946 Appointed Professor of Acting, National Drama School. Final version of *Nostalgia de la muerte* published by Mictlán.

1947 Productions of *El pobre Barba Azul* and *Invitación a la muerte* at the Palacio de Bellas Artes.

1948 Publication of *Canto a la primavera* by Stylo.

1949 Named Artistic Director of the annual programs of Mexican drama sponsored by the National Authors' Union.

1950 Performances of *La tragedia de las equivocaciones* at the Teatro del Caracol and *Juego Peligroso* at the Teatro Ideal. Publication by Nueva Voz of the edition of Torres Bodet's *Poemas.* Villaurrutia died of a coronary attack Dec. 25.

1951 First performance of *El Ausente* in the Palacio de Bellas Artes in a special program honoring Villaurrutia.

CHAPTER 1

The Man and His Time

I *The Background*

Xavior Villaurrutia was born into a Mexico which was to see during his life a political turmoil such as had not shaken the country since the wars of the Reform in the mid-nineteenth century, and a cultural transition which, in some ways, parallels this social ferment. The political stability, which most would prefer to call stagnation, of the regime of Porfirio Díaz, collapsed in 1910 under the pressure of economic and social injustice. From then until 1924, various factions struggled for political control in a bloodbath which saw the murders of Francisco I. Madero, leader of the revolt, and the most important Revolutionary chieftains, notably Pancho Villa, Emiliano Zapata, and Venustiano Carranza, who was president at the time of his assassination. Even after relative stability was achieved with the election of Plutarco Elías Calles in 1924, considerable turmoil continued, with the religious revolt known as the Cristero movement, the murder of President-Elect Obregón in 1928 and the repressive political measures of various national and regional political leaders. It was not until the election of Lázaro Cárdenas in 1934 and the expulsion of Calles by the new president in 1935 that public life in Mexico regained a substantial degree of stability and tranquillity, of respect for constitutional guarantees and the rights of the individual. Against this chaotic panorama, Villaurrutia lived the greater part of his life.

Although he took no part in political matters and appears to have been conservative in his political outlook, Villaurrutia was extremely active in the artistic activity which accompanied the political and social movements. The sterility of Díaz' government, which protected the rights and privileges of the wealthy few and cared little for the enormous masses of under-

privileged, many of whom lived in conditions of virtual slavery
in the rural areas, was also marked by a comparable sterility
in the educational system. By 1910, the National Preparatory
School, keystone of the system, was producing pedants without
the barest essentials of a humanistic system. As Alfonso Reyes
has pointed out, the humanities were ignored in favor of the
emphasis on technical education, but this technical education
reached only a tiny proportion of the population.[1] The prevail-
ing literary school was a decaying Modernism, whose cult of
France and love of color, music, and ornate decorativeness
fitted well into the framework of the Porfiriate. Such poets as
Manuel Gutiérrez Nájera (1859-95), Salvador Díaz Mirón
(1853-1928), and others were writers of the first rank, but their
art was a restricted one at best, and their followers lacked the
vigor to maintain the heights achieved by their leaders and the
initiative to develop their art in new directions.

The intellectual revolt against this atmosphere began in
1906, and in 1909 the group known as the Atheneum of Mexico,
under the leadership of Pedro Henríquez Ureña, a native of
Santo Domingo, developed a series of lectures which underlined
the intellectual unrest. Turning to the classical heritage of
Greece, to English and French literature, to the Spanish Golden
Age, the members of the Atheneum were instrumental in the
founding of the National University by Justo Sierra in 1910.
Shortly, the first Humanities faculty was established, and almost
all the appointments went to members of the Atheneum.

But these men, significant as they are, were, with a few
exceptions, not primarily creative artists. Their principal interest
was philosophy, and if their work caused a cultural revolt,
there were still few guides for the literary generation born
at the turn of the century. As students, young writers could
learn of the best of world culture while re-evaluating their
own national past; they could receive a solid grounding in the
severe discipline of the critical method. What they could not
find was guidance in their work as creative artists. Alfonso
Reyes was an important poet, but the classical serenity with
which he cloaked much of his work was hardly likely to attract
or influence younger poets, and the personal drama which
underlies much of his best work was invisible to younger men.
The novel suffered from acute debility. There were few authors

who could create a plot worthy of psychological development, and fewer still who could sustain characterization throughout a complete novel. The Novel of the Revolution had not yet appeared, and in any case, its strong political coloration would have held little interest for young writers primarily interested in esthetic values, while the work of older figures, such as the Catholic Naturalist Fernando Gamboa, seemed hopelessly out of date. The situation in the theater was worse; a few playhouses presented commercial Spanish works and inferior Mexican imitations, but a truly Mexican drama did not exist. The effect of the Porfiriate is best seen in the astonishing fact that there were more theaters in Mexico in 1859 than at any time since.[2]

Within this ill-defined literary panorama, younger men drifted without clear direction. The so-called Generation of 1915 was a promising group inspired by the ideals of the Atheneum, but its members, with the exception of Antonio Castro Leal, soon turned to other fields. The other two best-known members of the group are the archeologist Alfonso Caso and the politician Vicente Lombardo Toledano. About 1917, the group known as the Colonialists began to produce their fictional re-creation of Mexico's past, not in the spirit of critical reassessment of the Atheneum, who sought to understand their present through a better comprehension of the past, but rather as a flight from the bitterness and violence of the Revolution and possibly in part as an aftermath of World War I, which produced a literature of escapism and despair throughout the world. Although the Colonialists freed themselves in the next decade, and went on to become some of Mexico's best critics and creative artists, such as Genaro Estrada, Julio Jiménez Rueda, Ermilo Abreu Gómez, and Francisco Monterde, they remained under the influence of the past too long for them to be effective influences on the younger men.

There were in Mexico two poets of the first rank, although they were, and continue to be, little known outside Mexico: Enrique González Martínez, one of the few members of the Atheneum to concentrate on literature, and Ramón López Velarde. In what way did these men provide the challenge and inspiration for those younger poets who were eager to write, eager to follow the models they sought? We find the answer in Vill-

aurrutia's *La poesia de los jóvenes de México* (Young Mexican
Poetry). Of González Martínez, he says that while never before
in Mexican literature had such spiritual elevation and artistic
perfection appeared in the work of one man, González Martínez
was an impossible master precisely because his work was so
personal and of such spiritual integrity.[3] González Martínez
was, throughout his life, fundamentally a Symbolist, whose
poetry reflected his own personal preoccupations, his profound
commitment to the individual spirit. Such an influence, although
temporarily widespread, could only be closer to imitation than
absorption, and the best younger poets were too curious, too
restless, to settle for simple imitation; González Martínez' true
importance as a model lies in his singular devotion to poetry,
his insistence on a total commitment. Rather, Villaurrutia and
his contemporaries found their models in López Velarde and
the mercurial José Juan Tablada, one of the most underrated of
Mexican poets. The significance of the discovery of these two
most restless of poets can best be appreciated in Villaurrutia's
own formulation.

If Enrique González Martínez was, about 1918, the supreme and
almost the only god of our poetry; if the inspirations came from him,
if the young sang with their own lungs the personal pain of González
Martínez, in prayers similar to the tedious chorus which the angels
probably intone about God, we needed Adam and Eve to come again
to give us with their rebellion, with their sin, a land of our own, of
broader panoramas, of greater liberties, a land to see with our own
eyes. The formula is: Adam and Eve = Ramón López Velarde and
José Juan Tablada.[4]

Whether this formulation is in fact valid for all the members
of Villaurrutia's generation is debatable, but it is important
to recognize that these words were published when Villaurrutia
was twenty-one, while his poetry was still in a very formative
stage. López Velarde rejected the rationalism, the foreign spirit,
of the Atheneum; more important, his poetry is the expression
of the fundamental dualism of his own nature. He was a man
possessed by the angels and the devils, and the bulk of his
work is centered about the polarities of city and province, flesh
and soul, death and life; or, as he symbolized them, the figures
of two women, Fuensanta, the representative of purity and

the traditional virtues, and Sara, the embodiment of flesh and carnality. Even as Villaurrutia understood the basic nature of López Velarde's work—and he did so far earlier than most—he rejected the provincial element. While López Velarde was still widely imitated as a poet of provincial simplicity, Villaurrutia understood and learned from this poet of extreme technical and spiritual complexity. In the highly personal poetic language which López Velarde used to express his own spiritual world, Villaurrutia saw the importance of this uniqueness; in this sense, López Velarde is his technical master, while at the same time López Velarde taught the younger man that poetry could be the language of the poet's private and personal inferno without becoming sentimental or cheapened.

For Villaurrutia and his friends, Tablada represented eternal curiosity, perpetual awareness of new esthetic currents, constant experimentation with new forms and techniques. The whole of his work is, in a sense, a compendium of poetic currents during his lifetime. As a result of this eclectic virtuosity, Tablada has been overlooked as a mere dilettante, as a minor figure without real significance. He is, as Villaurrutia makes clear, one of the most perceptive figures of twentieth-century Mexican letters, deserving of greater study.

These two then, represented for many of the younger writers, and particularly for Villaurrutia, curiosity and awareness. López Velarde, the poet of the language of torment; Tablada, the poet of technique and curiosity; and, to some extent, González Martínez, the poet of the soul: these were the sources which set the younger men on the path of a vanguardist poetry of a highly personal sort.

II *The Man*

About Xavier Villaurrutia's personal life there is a pervasive mystery, as though this enigmatic personality had deliberately cultivated as a mode of existence those preoccupations which lie at the core of his plays and poetry. Those who were his friends refer repeatedly to the barriers which he interposed between his life as one of the most active members of his generation of Mexican letters, and the personal portion of his existence, into which few were permitted to enter. José Luis Martínez has specifically pointed out the manner in which

Villaurrutia kept his private life separate from his intellectual relationships.[5] This reluctance extended even as far as the date of his birth, which is given variously as 1903, 1904, 1905, and 1906, with an accompanying variety in months and days. This confusion has been compounded by the fact that his family and even Villaurrutia himself seem to have given different dates on different occasions. It is quite possible that the author, given his personal reserve and his mocking attitude toward such minutiae, did so deliberately. The most likely date seemed to be December 3, 1903, that given in the anthology *Ocho Poetas,* (Eight Poets), which includes his first poetry published in book form. This is also the date used by two of his closest friends, Salvador Novo and his personal physician Dr. Elías Nandino. However, in the posthumously published "Autobiography in Third Person" ("Autobiografía en tercera persona"),[6] he states that he was born on March 27, 1903, a date verified by the recent discovery of his birth certificate.[7]

Villaurrutia died of a coronary attack on Christmas Day, 1950, and even about this there is some mystery. Personal friends and, most importantly, Nandino, have stated that Villaurrutia had no medical history of cardiac illness; yet, throughout his work there are allusions which would seem to indicate some knowledge on his part of such a condition, or at the very least of a physiological predisposition to such illness. In his only published and, so far as is known, only complete novel *Dama de corazones* (Queen of Hearts), published in 1928, the narrator, Julio, makes the curious statement that he had been unable to enter military service because of a cardiac condition.[8] This could be entirely coincidental; however, given the fact that eleven pages later, Julio refers specifically to his supposed friend Xavier Villaurrutia and, in a lengthy word portrait, describes himself as identical to his friend, the coincidence becomes somewhat more startling, particularly since one of the characters in *Queen of Hearts* reads Julio's palm and refuses to tell him what she has seen in the heart line.[9] There are other coincidences, if such they be; and, for example, Rafael Solana seems to infer knowledge of such illness in his "Villaurrutia, poeta."[10] At this late date it would seem impossible to determine, but it would not have been atypical for this ironic and enigmatic individual who guarded so closely his personal existence, to have also guarded this fatal knowledge.

Villaurrutia's early life is symptomatic of the literary moment. The son of Rafael Villaurrutia and Julia González Casavantes de Villaurrutia, he was the nephew of Jesús Valenzuela, a minor Modernist poet and co-founder of the important *Revista Moderna*, the chief organ of Modernism from 1898 to 1911. Villaurrutia was educated at the Colegio Francés, the National Preparatory School, and the National School of Jurisprudence; this latter, as he put it, without enthusiasm.[11] Financially independent, he was able to abandon his legal studies after three years to devote himself to writing and to a self-imposed training in the humanities, which he felt had been neglected during his formal education. His earliest known poems were published in 1919, and he later characterized his verse of this period as poetry in which "the French Symbolists . . . left their music, their atmosphere and not infrequently their words."[12]

This is the period which saw the beginning of a close friendship with Salvador Novo and considerable literary activity. With Jaime Torres Bodet and Bernardo Ortiz de Montellano, Villaurrutia founded the review *La Falange* (1922-1923). He contributed, principally book reviews, to *Antena* (1924), and wrote the preface to Novo's translation of Francis Jammes's short stories, published in 1922. Several of his poems were included in the anthology *Ocho Poetas, 1923* (Eight Poets), and the following year *Antena* published his *Young Mexican Poetry*. In 1926, he published his first volume of poetry, *Reflejos* (Reflections). Meanwhile, he was employed in the Ministry of Health, and in 1928 obtained a position in the editorial department of the Ministry of Education.

Just prior to this latter employment, which was to prove important, Novo and Villaurrutia founded *Ulises*, a literary review devoted to the new ideas which the two discovered in their omnivorous reading. Although *Ulises* existed for only six issues, from May, 1927, to February, 1928, it attracted the attention of other young writers, and it is likely that the example of *Ulises* may have been in part responsible for the foundation of the review *Contemporáneos* and for Villaurrutia's employment in the Ministry of Education. Here he joined several other young writers who were to be the key members of the group which has come to be known as the "Contemporáneos" or "Contemporaries," after the journal which they published for several years, and who constituted what is certainly one of the most distinguished poetic movements in Latin American letters.

In his studies of the "Contemporáneos," Merlin Forster distinguished three subgroups. The first consists of Bernardo Ortiz de Montellano; Enrique González Rojo, son of González Martínez; José Gorostiza; and Jaime Torres Bodet. These four constituted the nucleus of the group, to which Villaurrutia and Novo and, finally, Jorge Cuesta and Gilberto Owen were later added. The original link was one of friendship and literary affinity, and Villaurrutia became a member of this loosely organized pleiade through his acquaintance with Torres Bodet, although he had known others earlier. In the same way, a number of other members of the same generation gravitated toward the group, such as Elías Nandino and Carlos Pellicer; although technically not members in the sense that they actively participated in the various literary reviews, especially *Contemporáneos*, they are part of the same general movement and must be so considered.

The first of the group to publish substantially was Pellicer, who was co-director with Octavio G. Barreda of the review *Gladios* in 1916. A year later, Torres Bodet began to contribute to *Pégaso*, whose chief contributors included López Velarde and González Martínez, as well as the outstanding Mexican exponent of the erotic poetry associated with the French "decadent" school, Efrén Rebolledo. These younger men also wrote extensively for reviews such as *Antena, La Falange,* and *México Moderno* (1920-1923). In 1928, they resolved to establish their own review, in the belief that Mexico needed a cosmopolitan literary periodical after the fashion of the *Nouvelle Revue Française* and *La Mercure de France* or the Spanish *Revista de Occidente*. The first number of *Contemporáneos* appeared in June, 1928, under the official direction of Torres Bodet, Ortiz de Montellano, González Rojo, and Bernardo Gastélum. The latter, although not primarily a literary figure, shared the group's ideas, and through his position as head of the Department of Health under President Calles, was able to ensure employment for his three co-directors and a subvention for the review. When, in December, 1928, Gastélum was not included in the new cabinet of President Portes Gil, a basic change took place in the direction of *Contemporáneos*. Gastélum, Torres Bodet and González Rojo accepted diplomatic posts in Europe, and during its remaining life the review was headed by Ortiz de Montellano, with considerable assistance from Genaro Estrada, Undersecretary of Foreign Affairs, who secured for Ortiz de Montellano a position as librarian.

Contemporáneos existed for forty-three numbers, from June, 1928, until December, 1931. After its cessation, the group maintained a relatively loose relationship for a number of years and collaborated on a number of important journals. However, they never again functioned as the voracious young intellectuals who had given Mexico one of its most important cultural periodicals. Much of the blame for the disappearance of the review and the subsequent dispersion of the group must be laid to the unrelenting persecution directed by literary nationalists who reflected the semiofficial literary line. The "Contemporáneos"' enemies created a dichotomy between their own nationalistic, naturalistic, "patriotic" literature, with a heavy social content, and the universalist, cosmopolitan esthetic orientation of Villaurrutia and his friends. Soon the dispute degenerated into a series of personal and journalistic attacks. In addition to the hostility generated by the contrast between the "Contemporáneos"' relatively hermetic and apolitical art and the socially committed, easily accessible and usually considerably inferior work of their enemies, there was also great resentment of the group's protection by Vasconcelos and Gastélum and the use of public funds to help finance their publications. The final provocation seems to have been the publication in 1928 of the *Antología de la poesía mexicana moderna* (Anthology of Modern Mexican Poetry) which bears Cuesta's name as editor, but which was prepared by the entire group. The *Anthology* was an effort to make better known the work of the group and at the same time to eliminate what the editors regarded as the undeserved reputations of previous poets. There is no question but that in this latter regard, it was heretical. At best premature, it may well have been ill-calculated. The resultant furor led to newspaper denunciations of the group, their review, and the affiliated theater group, Teatro Ulises, as un-Mexican. Some members of the "Contemporáneos" remained scornfully silent, which incensed their opponents still further, but even when Torres Bodet pointed out to the nationalists and propagandists that beauty can seldom be used for propagandistic purposes and remain beautiful,[13] the campaign continued.

The harassment did not restrict itself to literary polemics; Diego Rivera attacked the group in a public lecture because he disagreed with an article published in the first issue of *Contemporáneos,* and even painted an attack on them into his mural in the patio of the Ministry of Public Education. Finally, the campaign resulted in the picturesque incident of Rubén Salazar Mallén's novel, *Cariátide.* After the demise of *Contemporáneos,* in 1932, Cuesta began publication of a new review, *Examen,* in which he published the second chapter of *Cariátide.* The outraged press, still bitter at the group and doubly scandalized by the erotic nature of the work, forced the arrest of Cuesta and Salazar Mallén on a charge of outraging public decency. Although both were acquitted, *Examen* ceased publication, and the members of the group still occupying public positions were forced to resign. This marked the end of the group of "Contemporáneos" as such. It is an ironic commentary on the enmity and, perhaps, on its motivations, that among the young poets branded as reactionaries were several who have subsequently made important contributions to their people and their government in both public and private capacities.

It is not difficult to understand the vehemence of the attacks on the group, since they represent a thoroughly confused understanding of the relationship between art and politics. As John Brushwood has pointed out,[14] the cosmopolitan Europeanism of the "Contemporáneos" was identified by a militant wing of the social press and literary world as opposed to the nationalistic and nativist official stand. They saw the vanguardism of the "Contemporáneos," which admittedly, in some cases at least, had led to relatively hermetic works, as opposed to an art whose primary function was social and didactic and which had, therefore, to be easily accessible. The social commitment of the militants, who saw art as propaganda, perforce clashed with the esthetic commitment of the "Contemporáneos," who held a "clear concept of art as something substantive and transcendental."[15]

An extraordinary fact is that long after the heat of the moment had cleared, the same old charges were being leveled at the group. It is extraordinary because included among those attacked were figures such as Jaime Torres Bodet and José Gorostiza, who have rendered distinguished public service to their nation, and because the group has clearly established itself as one of the most important in Latin American literature in the twentieth century. Yet, we find Francisco González Guerrero saying in 1949 that "except for the most audacious or those of greatest personality, the "Contemporáneos" acted with a dilettantism such that not only did they not achieve originality, neither did they take root in Mexican form: this prevented their work from reaching the majority, which seemed to satisfy them, as they demonstrated by showing a real or feigned superiority, of which only a faction could boast. Nevertheless, we must not deny the talent of five or six, masters of great fantasy and creative force, whose work lasts and will last because of its high quality."[16] The inherent contradiction within this statement is clear when we realize that the group never included many more than six; González Guerrero's dislike for the group has led him to a blanket condemnation, from which he then grudgingly excepts nearly all the members on the basis of a literary ability which he has previously all but denied them. One of the more curious aspects of the entire polemic is the fact that they were repeatedly accused of being anti-Mexican, of ignoring their country's culture in favor of the culture of Europe and especially France. Yet, this is far from true. As Boyd Carter has pointed out in speaking of *Contemporáneos,* "The editors demonstrate extreme predilection for French letters and avant-garde literature. Nevertheless, it would be wrong to infer from the foregoing that in this outstanding literary review . . . national letters or the literary and intellectual expression of the Hispanic world are ignored. In the 43 substantial numbers of *Contemporáneos* are included many studies, articles, notes and documentation of considerable importance about Sor Juana, contemporary Mexican art, indigenous cultures, the theatre, recent Mexican books and other aspects of national life."[17]

Villaurrutia was one of the most active members of the group in the publication of *Contemporáneos* and contributed extensively: literary and art criticism, poetry and book reviews. His

interest in art was not incidental, nor was it exclusively critical;
he illustrated his own *Queen of Hearts* and, occasionally, the
work of friends, and in 1937 even had an exhibition of his own
work. Despite this considerable activity and the fundamentally
intellectual nature of most of his work, Villaurrutia was sufficiently human that he never became the pedant or the stock
character of the avant-garde poet. He was rescued by his sardonic sense of humor, as we see in this ironic self-portrait.

You would have me thus, proud, tall, loving, golden, capable of living
frenetic novels, capable of writing even more frenetic poems. You
are wrong. I suffer because I cannot please you. I imagine that you
cannot think of me as contemporary as Xavier Villaurrutia, as invisible as he, aspirant to diplomat, negligent in my dress; with a body
inclined more each day to disappear among the millions of young
men . . . ; with my loose-fitting suits, with my soft shirts, with the
movements of my head that accompany jazz . . . ; with my cigarettes
soaked in perfume, ephemeral, perfect. . . . Love me like this, friv-
olous, gay, with my concept of life and art as a distinguished sport
and nothing more.[18]

During the period of *Ulises,* Villaurrutia had become seri-
ously interested in the theater, an interest which was to become
the passion of his later life. The drama in Mexico was in a
deplorable state, despite a number of attempts at renovation,
such as the Group of Seven (1925) and, later, the Comedia
Mexicana (1929) and Teatro de Ahora (1932). Villaurrutia and
a group of his friends resolved to experiment with the theater,
and in 1928, Teatro Ulises (Ulysses Theater) was founded. The
theater itself was the salon of the home of Antonieta Rivas
Mercado, a wealthy woman of letters and sponsor of cultural
activities; seating capacity was fifty. Villaurrutia, Novo, Owen,
Celestino Gorostiza, brother of the poet José, Enrique Jiménez
Domínguez and Julio Jiménez Rueda doubled as actors and
directors. The actresses were Isabela Corona and Clementina
Otero; designers were Agustín Lazo, Roberto Montenegro,
Manuel Rodríguez Lozano, and Julio Castellanos. These men
recognized the decadence of the drama in Mexico, dependent
as it was on a decrepit Spanish model which was itself in
severe artistic straits; in Agustín Lazo's words, it was "the
deleterious routine of a false tradition."[19] The acting was a con-

scious imitation of what Villaurrutia called the Spanish school
of "improvisation and inspiration which we will call Romantic,
since it is necessary to call them something. . . ."[20] This decadent
imitation extended to the ludicrous extreme of requiring that
the actors, including Mexicans, imitate Spanish pronunciation.
The repertoire consisted of drawing-room comedies, melodramas,
and operettas, usually Spanish, or inferior Mexican imitations,
while the favorite genre was the slapstick farce.

The theaters themselves were in the same lamentable condition:

Where is the building which combines the indispensable conditions
to be a living theater, simple, aseptic, contemporary? Old houses or
vast amphitheaters, our theaters are almost always inadequate for the
spectacles which are put on in them.[21]

The typical producer, says the Spanish playwright Angel Lázaro,
was nothing more than a speculator, and Villaurrutia summed
up the situation thus:

Dirty theaters, old actors, anachronistic settings and impossible reper-
toires . . . behold the symptoms of the illness which is not strong
enough to put an end to the theater, but is acute enough to make it
drag out an existence covered with wounds, wounds covered with
rags.[22]

The motivating ideal of Teatro Ulises was relatively simple:
"Through new models, they sought to try out their own forces,
to create taste, a repertoire and new actors by participating
directly in the editing of the mysteries of the theatrical performance."[23] They realized that no significant theater movement can exist without actors capable of interpreting new artistic approaches and without a cultured public capable of ap-
preciating them. No such actors or public existed in Mexico,
so that one of the fundamental goals of Ulises was the training
of actors and the creation of a public. Where earlier experimental
groups had confined their experimentalism largely to mani-
festoes, while their own original efforts were within the framework of the accepted drawing-room comedy, Ulises presented
work by Dunsany, Roger-Marx, Vildrac, Cocteau, and O'Neill.
Heartened by their success before audiences of their friends,

they resolved to invade the commercial theater, with disastrous results. In spite of persistent attacks by the press, a manifestation of the mortal hatred in which these experimental artists were held by a radical and pedestrian press which echoed the official line of revolutionary reform and social art, Ulises staged several plays in the Fábregas Theater during the winter of 1928-29. Their failure was resounding, and they withdrew again to Antonieta Rivas Mercado's salon, where they staged one work by Lenormand and disbanded.

Despite this depressing experience, the group resolved to continue its efforts. In 1932, Celestino Gorostiza obtained permission to organize a training program for young actors under the patronage of the Ministry of Public Education. Despite this ostensible purpose, the new Teatro Orientación consisted primarily of those who had been connected with Ulises, and the principles remained the same, despite a greater formality of organization. There was a flat rejection of all compromise with current taste in the commercial theater; a certain amateur flavor was deliberately cultivated. Yet, Orientación prospered, and in 1933 the commercial stage was invaded once more. The repertoire was largely that which had been offered in the Ministry: O'Neill, Cocteau, Pellerin, Molière, Chekhov, Synge, Cervantes, Romains, Gogol, Shaw. During the professional period of 1933-34 and the final season of 1938, additions included Sophocles, Achard, Molnar, Lenormand, Behrman, Bontempelli, and Giraudoux. More important, new original work by members of the group were presented: Villaurrutia's *Parece mentira* (Incredible) and Gorostiza's *La Escuela del amor* (The School of Love) in the second 1933 season. Of the six works staged in 1934, four were Mexican: Villaurrutia's *¿En qué piensas?* (What Are You Thinking About?) Carlos Díaz Dufoo's *El barco* (The Ship) Alfonso Reyes' *Ifigenia Cruel* and Gorostiza's *Ser o no ser* (To Be or Not To Be). Although forced to suspend operations in 1935 because of a change in government policy, and the 1938 season was only a flicker of what had been done, Orientación proved that new Mexican plays could be successful and that the drama in Mexico could be more than deleterious routine.

Villaurrutia's role in this experimental theater was a major one. In addition to directing, he did a number of the translations and was responsible for the selection of many of the plays. Apparently, his influence went beyond even this; his personal magnetism attracted others of the same caliber to him, and he was, in the opinion of many critics, the central figure in much of the artistic activity of the period.

Xavier Villaurrutia was like a magnet. He had the gift of attracting to him and of communicating his dynamism to everyone, to all his friends, since every one of his collaborators became a friend of his in the very instant that the occasion came to work at his side. He could have filled the time of his precious existence by only devoting himself to increasing the volume of his crystalline verses, but Xavier did not hesitate to go out to meet a less individual task. His generosity had predestined him to be the coordinator of the majority of the artistic restlessness of his time.[24]

During this period of activity in the theater, Villaurrutia did not neglect other fields of artistic creation. In 1931, the first of his "Nocturnes" was published in the review *Barandal,* and two years later appeared in *Nocturnos* (Nocturnes), his first book since *Reflections.* This period also marks the publication of two major critical studies, the edition of Sor Juana Inés de la Cruz's sonnets in 1931 and the selected poems of López Velarde in 1935, with the introduction which is the source of the critical re-evalution of the poet of Fuensanta. In 1937, two new nocturnes appeared in book form, and the same year *La Pintura Mexicana Moderna* (Modern Mexican Painting) was published in Barcelona. The following year, Ediciones Sur of Buenos Aires published the first edition of *Nostalgia de la muerte* (Nostalgia of Death), his major poetic work.

Despite this activity in poetry and criticism, the drama occupied more and more of Villaurrutia's efforts. He spent 1935 studying at the Yale Drama School under a grant from the Rockefeller Foundation; upon his return to Mexico, he founded in 1936 the drama group of the Electricians' Union and was its director until 1939. The list of productions reflects the same challenging interest in European drama: Schnitzler, Romains, Vildrac, and Chekhov, as well as his own *Incredible* and *What Are You Thinking About?* When Celestino Gorostiza was named to organize a new drama group for the Department of Fine Arts, he appointed Villaurrutia, Julio Bracho, and Rodolfo Usigli professors of dramatics.

The remaining decade of Villaurrutia's life continued this
varied activity. In poetry, he published in 1941 *Décima muerte*
(Death in Tenths) incorporated five years later into the definitive edition of *Nostalgia of Death*. In 1948, appeared the last
volume of poetry, *Canto a la primavera* (Song to Spring), although several important poems were published in reviews
during the following two years. This is also the period of
Villaurrutia's development as a professional playwright; after the
five *Autos Profanos* (Worldly Allegories), his first commercial
play *La Hiedra* (The Ivy) was staged in 1941; the next year
La mujer legítima (The Legitimate Wife) received second prize
in a contest for Mexican plays sponsored by the Ideal Theater.
This award provoked a series of outbursts by critics who com-
plained heatedly that the work was entirely commercial and a
betrayal of the ideals of Ulises and Orientación. Certainly, it is
true that *The Legitimate Wife* is a far way from the *Worldly
Allegories* and employs a number of stock devices of the professional theater. At the same time, it must be remembered that
these devices are not used entirely as they were in the commercial
drama, and there is some indication that they were used deliberately in ironic fashion. Second, Villaurrutia's purpose was,
after all, to demonstrate that straightforward commercial drama
could be written with style and quality. Whatever the weak-
nesses of the play, he made his point, and the work's success
established him as one of Mexico's most important dramatists. In
1943, his best and most provocative play, *Invitación a la muerte*
(Invitation to Death), written some years earlier, was staged
with little success; a recasting of the Hamlet theme into Mexican
terms, it was too advanced for its time. The following year,
Villaurrutia returned to the theater of character in realistic
psychological terms with *El yerro candente* (The Burning Error).
The year 1947 saw the premiere of his only full-length comedy,
El pobre barba azul (Poor Bluebeard), and his last play, *Juego
peligroso* (Dangerous Game) was staged shortly before his death.

    In addition to this activity within the professional theater,
Villaurrutia continued to experiment with the one-act play in
El solterón (The Bachelor), an unstaged version of Schnitzler's
Der Tod das Junggesellen and *La Tragedia de las equivocaciones*
(The Tragedy of Errors), a monodrama performed in 1950. He
also wrote a number of filmscripts and twice received the Ariel

for screenwriting, corresponding to the American Oscar. With Agustín Lazo, he wrote the book and lyrics for J. Pablo Moncaya's operetta *La mulata de Córdoba* (The Mulato Girl of Cordoba). He also continued to be active as a director, and was, with Celestino Gorostiza and Paco Fuentes, involved in the staging of many of the works performed during the three seasons of productions of the group, The Theater of Mexico, 1943-1945. In 1946, he was named professor of acting at the newly founded School of Dramatic Arts of the National Institute of Fine Arts, and three years later was appointed artistic director of the series of annual programs of Mexican drama established in that year by the National Author's Union.

In addition, Villaurrutia continued his activities as a critic and taught at the summer sessions of the National University. A series of editions included Sor Juana's *Endechas* (1940), her *Sonetos y endechas* (1941), and a selection of López Velarde's work entitled *El león y la virgen* (1942). From the same period are *Textos y pretextos* (Texts and Pretexts) (1940), a selection from his many essays of criticism, and *Laurel* (1941), an anthology of modern poetry in Spanish prepared in collaboration with Octavio Paz, Emilio Prados, and Juan Gil-Albert; one of its best features is Villaurrutia's discerning prologue. He also contributed extensively to literary reviews such as *Letras de México, Tierra Nueva, Romance, Rueca* and the *Revista de Guatemala;* in 1943, he was again associated with Octavio G. Barreda in the foundation of the important literary review, *El Hijo Pródigo.* In addition to writing forty-two collaborations of various sorts, he was a member of the editorial board for the first twenty-nine numbers and was editor for the last thirteen. He also served as director of the publishing series New Collection Culture and wrote many of the introductions for its editions of Mexican and European authors, while translating Duhamel's *Dans l'ombre des statues,* Lenormand's *L'ombre du mal,* Giraudoux's *Judith* and *La guerre de Troie n'aura pas lieu,* Pirandello's *La giara* and *La vita che te diedi,* and sections of Morand's *Nouvelle visite à l'Amérique.* At the time of his death, he was preparing a new review with Alfonso Reyes, the poetess Guadalupe Amor, and his longtime friend, Elías Nandino, and he was engaged in writing a play on the Empire of Iturbide, the manuscript of which appears to have been lost.

I Reflections and the Early Poems

Villaurrutia's first published poems appeared in periodicals; the earliest known are from 1919. They betray a clear influence of González Martínez, whose influence is also visible, mixed with echoes of López Velarde, in works such as "With a Humble Glance . . ." ("Con la mirada humilde . . .," 1921). Generally, they are orthodox in style and content, with little indication of the highly original development which was to characterize the mature work. Their melancholy was probably rather more due to Villaurrutia's admitted reading of Samain, Jammes and other Symbolists, as well as López Velarde, whose vocabulary is clearly visible in several, than to any real personal commitment. "*Tarde*" (Evening), "*La bondad de la vida*" (The Goodness of Life), "*Antes*" (Before), "*Bajo el sigilo de la luna*" (Beneath the Reserve of the Moon), "*En el agua dormida*" (In the Sleeping Water) have in common the humble pleasures of life, with lines such as "There is sweetness in the soul, and youth, and life,) and perfume in the evening . . ."[7] or "A humble truth as rest,/ a peaceful silence, a loved book. . . ."[8] The same mood is expressed in amorous terms in "*Canción apasionada*," (Passionate Song), which is far more nostalgic than passionate, or "*Lamentación de primavera*" (Spring Lament). This melancholy achieves greater profundity in poems such as "*Más que lento*," (More Than Slow), in which the pressure of the beloved's hand confers tranquillity, but at the same time the young poet feels as though he is "in the aged chiaroscuro/ of a melancholy portrait. . . ."[9]

These poems are clearly more learned than profoundly felt; their melancholy wears the words of other poets. There are several, however, which are of greater importance. The two best are "*Ya mi súplica es llanto*" (Now My Plea Is Tears) and "*Ni la leve zozobra*" (Not the Slight Suffering), both of which bear the clear imprint of López Velarde's vocabulary, but are considerably less bookish and more tightly constructed than the others. The last stanza of the latter, particularly, achieves a tense, crabbed expression not unworthy of the model. Both poems express in religious terms a growing sense of estrangement, and it is significant that the plea for faith of the first and the grateful acceptance of this gift of the second, are the

last specifically religious formulations of the poet's alienation
for more than twenty-five years. Whatever personal religious
beliefs he may have held, Villaurrutia's mature poetry demonstrates the opposite pole from this peace and acceptance. There
is in few of these early works any real hint of the anguish and
the concentration on death of the later poems, and the occasional
appearance of such key later terms as "bedroom," the suggestion
of the *Reflections* in "Midnight," the conventional references to
death, which are often remarked as antecedents, are hardly
more than coincidental. Only in *"Presentimiento"* (Present-
ment), *"Canción"* (Song) or *"La visión de la Lluvia"* (The Vision
of the Rain) do we find a suggestion of the anguish of *Nostalgia
of Death.*

Reflections (1926) is a product of the vogue of "pure" poetry,
and particularly Juan Ramón Jiménez' persistent efforts to arrive
at a quintessential poetry, with the elimination of narrative,
anecdote, and other supposedly nonpoetic factors. The volume
consists of a series of brief lyrics, and as the title suggests, they
are reflections of the external world, sensory impressions ele-
vated to an abstract plane, in the poet's effort to create an
objective portrait, without being personally involved in his
creation. Eduardo Colín has pointed out how appropriate is
the title to this fusion of painting and literature, in which life
is "focused as in a picture . . .,"[10] and Alberto R. Lopes calls
the *Reflections* still lifes in the style of Cezanne.[11] There is a
good deal of truth in these observations; *"Aire"* (Air) is in
large measure an objective portrait of the atmosphere and the
tricks it plays on human perceptions of color, sound, and distance. *"Jardín"* (Garden) is a reflection of a spring garden, and
"Pueblo" (Village) a portrait of a village left desolate when its
inhabitants went off to fight. Indeed, three of the poems are
entitled *"Cuadro"* (Portrait), "Interior" and "Cezanne." But the
parallel should not be pushed too far, since the seeming ob-
jectivity of many of the poems does not hide a strong note of
melancholy. In *"Sueño"* (Dream), the poet wonders whether
the lovers will be joined in life as they were in the dream,
and in *"Noche"* (Night), they are so stricken by the approaching separation that the moment of passion becomes a simple
"Let us love, if you wish . . ." ("Gocemos, si quieres . . ."). At
times, this melancholy becomes an overwhelming ennui; the

world seen from a hilltop is a "Puzzle" not worth arranging. Or it is a colorless nothingness, a total lack of affirmation *"Incolor"* (Colorless). The melancholy becomes sharper as the sense of solitude grows, a solitude which overpowers as it follows from the eyes of the woman in the portrait *"Soledad"* (Solitude). The poet would flee the village "so that Sunday/ would come behind the train/ pursuing me . . ." ("Sunday"),[12] flee the silence which "has crumpled us,/ useless, in the corners" ("Phonographs").[13] Just as these lines are a clear anticipation of the hallucinated flight of the nocturnes, in *"Amplificaciones"* (Amplifications) the silence becomes a living menace which predicts the horror of the later poems.

> And the silence moves
> and vibrates
> about the soft flame,
> like the wing—of what omen?
> of what insect?—which caresses,
> which cools, which diminishes.[14]

And the solitude grows about him.

> The solitude grows
> like the shadows
> on the sheet of the wall,
> like the faces of yesterday . . .[15]

The increasing importance of this theme even at this early stage is shown by Chumacero's affirmation that Villaurrutia's favorites from *Reflections* were *"Calles"* (Streets), "Solitude," "Portrait," and "Amplifications,"[16] which are among those poems which most clearly foreshadow the steady emergence of the major themes of solitude and death.

Among the best of the *Reflections* are the eight brief lyrics of the *"Suite del insomnio"* (Insomniac's Suite), a group of haiku. Originally a Japanese verse form which appeared in the seventeenth century, the haiku are normally composed of three lines of five, seven, and five syllables, whose principal esthetic concentration is the effort to capture a momentary perception of significance or beauty. There have been at least

two distinct waves of interest in the haiku in Mexico, among
the Modernists and in the poetry of Tablada, and Villaurrutia's
interest probably stems from the latter's use of the form, although Juan Ramón Jiménez, who influenced virtually every
member of Villaurrutia's generation during their formative
years, cultivated forms which sometimes resemble the haiku
closely. In any event, the rigid structure of the model was
relaxed in Spanish to include two, three, or four lines of seven
to nine syllables, although the insistence on pure imagery is
retained.

"Insomniac's Suite" includes several poems which are haiku
in almost the purest sense, such as *"Eco"* (Echo)—"Night plays
with the noises/ copying them in her mirrors/ of sounds"[17]
and *"Alba"* (Dawn)—"Slow and violet/ she puts rings under
the glasses/ and the glance."[18] There is, however, in several, a
further anticipation of the themes and techniques of *Nostalgia
of Death.* The *"Tranvías"* (Streetcars) which "run mad/ with
fire, fleeing/ from themselves,/ among the skeletons of the
others/ immobile . . ."[19] are very nearly the germ of a nocturne,
and there are technical devices which later play an important
role, such as the transposition of terms in *"Lugares. I"*
(Places. I):

> Let us go, unmoving, on a trip
> to see the evening of always
> with another glance,
> to see the glance of always
> with a different evening.
>
> Let us go, unmoving.[20]

This is not simple playing with words; it is not only the same
old afternoon, it is the same old look. Both externally and
internally, the poet finds the same lack of meaning; it is not
accident that the word "empty" should occur so frequently
throughout. Another typical note is the use in "Phonographs" of
the following figure:

> And the heart,
> the heart of mica
> —without diastole or sistole—
> goes mad beneath the needle
> and bleeds its past in cries.[21]

Villaurrutia's frequent references to the heart have been referred to in the previous chapter, but here we have the first
clear use of medical terminology, and the suffering evoked by
the playing of the record is at least suggested to be equivalent
to the suffering of a surgical operation.

The imagery of *Reflections* presents a remarkable insistence
on concretion and depersonalization. The personality of others
is "the metal of reflections . . .";[22] time is ". . . the metal of the in-
stants. . . ."[23] Memory becomes a mirror of silence in which to
survey the past (Air), and nude bodies take on the sheen of
fine wood (Night). Moonlight is ". . . this white dust . . .,"[24] the
atmosphere a glass barrier between eyes and landscape (Air).
Further, this process is reflected in the poet himself; his ear
is the ". . . . shell of hearing . . .,"[25] filled with ". . . silver echoes
of water . . ."[26] (Air). His heart is mica (Phonographs), his
voice a hidden record (Streets), and the memory of the depart-
ing lover is caught on ". . . the plate of my retina."[27]

There is also considerable use of inversion and antithesis. The
nude bodies of "Night" take on the sheen of fine wood, but they
also become opaque, and in the same poem, dawn is a bottomless
pit, not of darkness but of light. The air which returns from a
voyage ". . . full of golden heat/freezes . . .,"[28] and of water the
poet asks no more taste "than that it have no taste. . . ."[29]

These techniques, like the insistence on echoes, walls, mirrors, streets and other recurrent terms, are sometimes only hinted
in *Reflections,* but they crystallize in the later volumes. The
preoccupation with concrete materials and attributes as symbols
of the poet's state of mind is a manifestation, or perhaps we
should say an inversion, of his growing concern with questions
which were to become the focus of *Nostalgia of Death.* An
increasing sense of solitude led him to grope for symbols which
demonstrated his union with external reality; at the same time,
walls and mirrors began to reflect his alienation. The human
beings become depersonalized, and the poet seems to communicate best with inanimate beings. As Jorge Cuesta pointed
out, in Villaurrutia's preoccupation with external form in his
search for identification, he became a mirror reflecting outward
all that he perceived.[30]

Perhaps the most important poem of this period is *"Poesía"*
(Poetry), written in 1927 just after the publication of *Reflections;*

Villaurrutia has said that had it been completed in time, it
should have appeared as the first poem in the volume.[31] He
called it the ars poetica of *Reflections,* and it is the only poem
of its sort he wrote. In "Poetry," Villaurrutia speaks to his art
directly in terms which are startlingly close to those which he
would later use to speak to his inseparable companion, Death.
"You àre the company with whom I speak/ suddenly, àlone."[32]
This is a poetry formed of "the words which emerge from
silence . . .,"[33] an introspective poetry formed more and more of
the poet's internal world, a poetry which surges from the "tank
of sleep in which I drown/ free until I awake."[34] It is obvious
that despite the poet's statements, "Poetry" demonstrates a clear
tendency away from the semiobjective poems of *Reflections*
and toward the obsessive themes of *Nostalgia of Death.* Further,
if Villaurrutia indeed felt that it represented his creative process
during the period of the *Reflections,* it demonstrated the co-
herence of his esthetic, since it clearly represents the same approach as that expressed in the interview with José Luis Martínez
some years later. In both instances, the poet quite clearly has
no control over the act of creation; in "Poetry," the poem
gradually appears to him, even in sleep, until it is fully formed.
Even admitting Villaurrutia's repeated stress on the role of the
intellect in poetry and his undeniable control of the finished
form, this is very close indeed to the Surrealists, and there is
more than a hint of their automatic writing in the second verse.

> Your metallic hand
> hardens my hand's hurry
> and leads the pen
> which traces on the paper its shore.[35]

Curiously, the identical notion is applied to Death in one of
the best of the later poems, *"Nocturno en que habla la muerte"*
(Nocturne in Which Death Speaks). The similarity is heightened
by the use in "Poetry" of a technical trick which characterizes
many of the later works, and which is all but nonexistent in
Reflections. This is paronomasia, or similarity of sounds, here
exemplified by the repeated *oz* in "Tu voz, hoz de eco" ("Your
voice, sickle of echo"), by the play between "por mil Argos"
("through a thousand Argos") and "por mí largos" ("long for

me"). Another example is the repetition "sin más cara,/ sin máscara . . ." ("with no more face,/ without a mask"). To what extent this word play is a momentary surrender to automatic writing is impossible to determine, but that it is much more is undeniable, in spite of somewhat less than careful critics who have seen in these usages simple games, verbal and aural trickery. The extent to which they were in error in this and the extent to which such verbal deftness enriches some of Villaurrutia's finest work will be seen later, but even here it is obvious that he is not simply playing games. The function of paronomasia is to establish an illogical, rather than a logical, association. The voice of poetry is a sickle of echoes in that it resumes past experience, allusion and suggestion, all the multiple echoes which produce the poetic word. The "mil Argos— mí largos" paronyms have an obvious function; the reference is clearly to the Argonauts and their encounter with the one-eyed giant, Cyclops. The allusion to a personage whose chief identification is through his single staring eye reinforces the preceding "I am watching myself watch me" ("me estoy mirando mirarme"); the poet becomes transfixed by his own stare, and the seconds, understandably, become very long indeed. The same function is visible in "más cara—máscara"; he is left without pulse or voice or face, that is, without individuality, since this is conferred by the act of poetic creation. The poet exists as poet in function of his poem. But when this transpires, he is left too without his mask, reduced to the defenseless self.

"Poetry" is, then, remarkably close in both theme and technique to the later work. To what extent Villaurrutia consciously identified his fundamental theme with poetry and art, to what extent "Nocturne in which death speaks" may have been modeled on "Poetry," we cannot say. It is clear, however, that they were somehow related for him, and "Poetry" proves for us that as early as 1927, when he had just published a volume which is usually considered to be totally different from his mature work, this identification of form and substance was already developed.

II   Queen of Hearts

In 1928, Villaurrutia published *Queen of Hearts,* a brief prose narrative which is included here because its values are

not those of the novel or novelette as we know them. Although
he appears to have written others,[36] this is the only complete
prose work extant. *Queen of Hearts* is a minor work, within a
genre abandoned thereafter by the author, but it is of interest
largely because of a number of lyrical passages which are virtually poetry arranged in prose form, and for its anticipation in
embryonic form of themes which were not fully developed until
the mature poetry and plays. Villaurrutia has clarified his purpose in an article published only recently. "The text of *Queen
of Hearts* does not attempt to be that of a novel nor achieve
anything more than what I proposed that it be; an interior
monologue in which I followed the consciousness of a character
during a precise real time and during a psychic time conditioned
by the conscious reflections, by the emotions and by the real or
invented dreams of the protagonist who, in spite of expressing
himself in the first person, is not necessarily I. . . . At the same
time, *Queen of Hearts* attempted to be an exercise in dynamic
prose, prickly with metaphors, agile and light, like that which
Giraudoux or, more modestly, Pierre Girard cultivated, like an
image of the time in which it was written."[37]

Queen of Hearts is one of a series of experimental short
novels written by the "Contemporáneos" during the late 1920's
and early 1930's under the influence of Giraudoux, Proust, and
possibly Joyce. These experimental works were a reaction to
the mediocrity and vulgarity of the usual novel, sheer action and
anecdote, to the flight toward Spain visible in the work of
Alfonso Reyes, to the mannered interest in the colonial period
which occupied many novelists.[38] It shows the same preoccupation with material substance which we have seen in *Reflections*
and which is to become a constant technique in *Nostalgia of
Death*. In description, there is a constant emphasis on specific
detail, on exact shadings of color and exact properties of fabrics.

> . . . I look at the study draped in somber
> green.[39]

> The light . . . is tinted softly in the glass
> and in the curtains of light cretonne.[40]

There is the same concretion in the image.

> . . . a splendid day which you are to slice and
> enjoy like a ripe fruit. . . .[41]

> . . . that watery tunnel of the years, which can
> at last drown you. . . .[42]

> The sound of my steps comes out to meet me
> rejected by the walls.[43]

The plot of *Queen of Hearts* is so simple as to be tenuous. Julio, a Mexican student in the United States, has returned to Mexico for a holiday to visit his aunt and his barely remembered cousins Aurora and Susana. During the visit the aunt dies, and Julio leaves. This nearly transparent narrative is simply a frame for the themes, the virtual identity of Aurora and Susana. Although initially they are indistinguishable for him, he soon recognizes differences of personality which intrigue him greatly; where Aurora is reserved, Susana is highly emotional. Aurora is engaged to a man whom she does not love, and Julio begins to fall in love with Susana, whether from preference or simply opportunity is not clear. His departure leaves the reader with only rapid impressions of two nearly identical personalities who perhaps hide beneath their similarities very different natures. Or perhaps these differences are the superficial level, and beneath they are indeed identical. This theme returns in *The Tragedy of Errors* in which Villaurrutia toys with the concept of identical twins of very different natures, and the sometimes crippling, sometimes ribald confusion to which their identical appearance leads.

Another antecedent of a later play is the scene in which Julio ventures into a funeral agency; the entire scene is an obvious early version of the setting for the play *Invitation to Death*. More important, however, is the death theme which is here more fully developed than in *Reflections*. Although not yet the seductively fatal mistress of *Death in Tenths*, death is present.

It is not difficult to die. I had already died, in life, a few times. Everything depends on not making a single movement, on not saying a single word, on fixing one's eyes on a point, near, far. Above all, on not being distracted by a thousand things.[44]

This astonishing passage is part of a dream sequence which occupies more than a tenth of the story. In itself, it is a fascinating incursion into a region where perspectives are changed and familiar objects strangely altered. It may destroy what little narrative exists, and the limits of the dream are not entirely defined; the reader is never completely a part of the dream because he is left suspended between dream and reality. Nevertheless, in the passage quoted we find a clear anticipation of the major themes of the later work, and the closing of the passage is very close to being a poem in itself.

Dying is equivalent to being nude, on a divan of ice, on a hot day, with one's thoughts directed to a single target which does not spin like the target of the ingenuous marksmen who lose their fortune at the fair. Dying is being happily out of communication with people and things, and looking at them as the lens of a camera must look, with exactitude and coldness. Dying is no more than becoming a perfect eye which looks without becoming emotional.[45]

III Nostalgia of Death

Villaurrutia's highest poetic achievement was published in definitive form in 1946; it is a radical intensification of themes hinted at in the earlier work. The relatively objective reproduction of the external world has disappeared entirely, and the nostalgic loneliness is here a livid nightmare of anguished solitude. In the desperate lucidity of the night, the poet faces the horror of existence, a horror compounded of absolute isolation and the inevitable presence of death. Octavio Paz has described this work in a review of the 1938 edition as "his own death, which he cultivates like a terrible personal plot of land with the same passion and fever with which others construct their long ruinous lives . . . and on cultivating his death, his like his love, like his solitary desire, he has cultivated his life, creating it there where his death dwells. . . ."[46]

The 1946 edition includes the three sections "*Nocturnos*" (Nocturnes), "*Otros nocturnos*" (Other Nocturnes), to which Chumacero has added the poem "When the Evening" ("Cuando la tarde"), and a section entitled "Nostalgias." The first two are substantially alike and may logically be treated as the major portion of the work, while the last includes several poems rather different in spirit and the splendid sequence, *"Décima muerte"* (Death in Tenths). "Nocturnes" is preceded by a line from the sonnet sequence "Idea" of the Elizabethan poet, Michael Drayton (1563-1631): "Burned in a sea of ice, and drowned amidst a fire." It is significant that Villaurrutia chose such a baroque antithetical line, since, aside from his own predilection for such verses, this frustration raised to a metaphysical level, the despairing effort to express the inexpressible, is precisely what he here attempts. The world of *Nostalgia of Death* is a nocturnal world in which all that is real has vanished, and we are besieged by shadows, menacing figures, distorted shapes, in a universe gone mad. In this desperate solitude, the poet asks repeatedly who and what he is. Unable to establish meaningful contact with anyone, he doubts his own existence.

> And who among the shadows of a deserted street,
> in the wall, livid mirror of solitude,
> has not seen himself pass or come to meet
> and has not felt fear, anguish, mortal doubt?
>
> The fear of being only an empty body
> which someone, I myself or any other, can occupy,
> and the anguish of seeing oneself outside, living,
> and the doubt of being or not being reality.[47]
>
> ("Fear Nocturne")

In the mystery of the night, the poet has become a disembodied intellect, unable to find one who might say to him, "I see you, ergo, you exist." Wherever he looks, he sees only himself reflected in walls, in the faces of passersby, until he doubts his own being. This theme is obsessive; in *"Nocturno grito"* (Cry Nocturne), he asks:

> Can that be my shadow
> disembodied, which passes?
> And mine the lost voice
> which goes setting fire to the street?[48]

Existence is, for Villaurrutia, this search for identification; even in his theater, as we shall see, a hallucinated flight through empty streets in search of meaning. *"Nocturno solo"* (Nocturne Alone) is almost a definition of this void.

Solitude, boredom,
vain profound silence,
liquid shadow in which I sink,
vacuum of the thought.[49]

In the last line, he completes the definition: "this invisible ship-wreck."[50] The same theme is developed at greater length in *"Nocturno eterno"* (Eternal Nocturne), a description of the utter desolation of this life without life. When men shrug their shoulders and pass by, when a dust finer even than smoke adheres to the crystal of the voice, when the eyes close their windows which look into the rays of the prodigal sun (!) and prefer blindness to pardon and silence to the sob, it is the time when life. "or what we call thus uselessly . . ."[51] chooses death by drowning in alcohol or by fire in the snow. It is the moment when man makes the inevitable choice between a desperate hedonism and an even more desperate intellectualism. It is the moment when life longs to cease, when forgotten stars shine in a dead sky, when a sudden cry leaves behind a blinding silence which is more silent for having been broken. It is the moment when all has died, so slowly that one is afraid to make a sound for fear of hearing no answer. Man is afraid to answer the mute question lest he learn that he no longer exists, that the voice is only a memory in the throat, and night the eternal blindness of a living death.

. . . because life silence skin and mouth
and solitude memory sky and smoke
are nothing but shadows of words
which come to meet us in the night.[52]

The uninterrupted, unpunctuated series emphasizes the opaque, almost solid darkness through which the poet struggles.

The "Other Nocturnes" are in the same vein. *"Nocturno"* (Nocturne) describes the moment before sleep, the long awaited and yet feared moment before the dream becomes real and reality disappears.

At last the night arrived to waken words
alien, unused, one's own, vanished. . . .[53]

And becomes silent, and the senses are heightened.

> The slightest sound grows suddenly and, then,
> dies without agony.[54]

The poet sleeps and is drawn into the shadow of the dream.

> And it is useless to light a lamp at my side:
> the light makes deeper the mine of silence
> and through it I descend, unmoving, from myself.[55]

He sink into the ancient ocean,

> . . . sea of an ancient dream,
> of a dream hollow and cold in which nothing now remains
> of the sea except the remains of a shipwreck of oblivions.[56]

This is the true significance of the dreams, for in them all the torment of the day lives a doubly hideous and yet compellingly attractive reality.

> Because the night drags on its low tide
> anguished memories, congealed fears,
> the thirst for something which, trembling, we drank one day,
> and the bitterness of what we no longer remember.[57]

Again, the repetition of symbol: the night is a pit into which the poet descends or a low tide choked with half-forgotten memories. These symbols and the constant disassociation of natural phenomena from the senses which normally perceive them are essential techniques in Villaurrutia's attempt to express the nightmare quality of his vision.

In "*Nocturno mar*" (Sea Nocturne), Villaurrutia uses the sea-motif to develop further his preoccupation with solipsism, the eternal and absolute solitude of the individual. The sea here is the poet's inability to break through the restrictions of his own personality, "the sea ancient Oedipus. . . ."[58] This curious and, given the basic themes of Villaurrutia's plays, certainly conscious equation of the Oedipus complex with the attempt to establish some kind of human relationship, is one of the few references to external, objective myth in the poems, although the plays are in their majority reassessments or reinterpretations of mythological or archetypal forms. In "Sea Nocturne," at least in the womb, there is total identification with another, even though it requires complete submersion of the individual personality. The sea, thus, is simultaneously the whole ebb tide of detritus which seals us within our own psyches—the level on which it functions throughout the poem—and the only solution to the problem, abandonment of self—a secondary level of significance.

There is an unusual amount of alliteration in "Sea Nocturne," frequently concentrated on harsher consonants; there is also a considerable use of paronomasia. Perhaps the most arresting portion of the poem, however, is the last verse, whose understatement underlines the despair of the previous verses. Recognizing the impossibility of any satisfactory resolution, the poet speaks of his agony almost tenderly.

> I carry it within me like remorse,
> alien sin and mysterious dream,
> and I soothe it and I lull it
> and I hide it and I care for it and I keep its secret.[59]

This solipsistic anguish is given a further dimension in "*Nocturno amor*" (Love Nocturne), the impossibility of maintaining more than momentary communication. The moment of passion over, the lovers lie quietly, each deep within the rigid confines of his own personality: "next to your body deader than dead/ which is your body no longer but only its void. . . ."[60] This is the form which love takes, after the spasmodic moment is irretrievably lost, in nearly all Villaurrutia's poetry. There is no longer any contact, and the lover's body is *hueco*, empty space, the hollow left behind, devoid of meaning. At the same time, reinforcing the dreadful realization of their inability to break down the walls between them, it is an *eco*, a memory of what can never be more than a fragmentary relief. Each is doomed, locked forever within his own mind, forever "the statue which wakes/ in the alcove of a world which has died."[61]

"*Nocturno de la alcoba*" (Nocturne of the Bedroom) fuses this solipsistic despair with the presence of death. Death is inherent in the form of the objects in the room and raises a cold, crystalline wall between them; it is the hollow left by her body when she rises, another of Villaurrutia's obsessive metaphors of the double agony of the realization that for an instant they have almost broken the barrier. This love is not so much a physical or spiritual mating as a mutual desire to establish contact or at least to find that the other understands. It is *this* need which is unfulfilled, and they are left "more than alone and shipwrecked, /still more, and more each time, still."[62]

The only bitter possibility of identification is expressed in "*Estancias nocturnas*" (Nocturnal Stanzas). The poet wanders the streets of the "submerged city,"[63] awake and yet dreaming: "And I doubt! And I do not dare to wonder if the awakening from a dream or the dream is my life."[64] The echoes of his footsteps are perhaps only the echoes of other steps; perhaps his steps have no sound. Perhaps, even, there are no steps; perhaps he does not even exist.

> The fear of being only a shred of the dream
> of someone—of God?—who dreams of this bitter world.
> The fear he may awaken, this someone—God?—the lord
> of a dream forever longer and more profound.[65]

The fear is heightened by the double nature of the Spanish *sueño,* which may mean either sleep or dream, so that while the first line clearly expresses the poet's fear that he may be only the fragment of another's dream, in the last line this dream is simultaneously a deeper and even longer sleep, thus dooming the poet to an even deeper and unending anguish.

The stars, like the poet, are cold and dead, but they, at least, have the consolation that their light is visible still, while he can be only "dust in the dust and oblivion in the oblivion!"[66] Despairing, he grasps for the only shred of identification with another, in a direct allusion to González Martínez' "*Mañana los poetas*" (Tomorrow the Poets), completing the circle by identifying himself with the man he once called an impossible master.

> But someone, in the anguish of an empty night,
> without knowing it, he or I, someone not yet born
> will speak with my words his nocturnal agony.[67]

This is no Romantic search for immortality in the afterlife or in the consolation of the eternal cycle of matter. The poet can only hope for the anonymous immortality of the community of suffering.

These are intellectual preoccupations, a conscious investigation of a philosophical dilemma which distresses contemporary thinkers and creative artists. This interest has frequently caused Villaurrutia to be labeled an Existentialist. As we shall see, there is some community of interest, but such labeling fails to take into account certain vital differences. For Villaurrutia, this dilemma is an absorbing passion which blurs the distinction between modes of existence and which finds perhaps its higher expression in the area between sleeping and waking. Not only does he wander in a nightmarish nocturnal world; he becomes part of this world and exists in a realm where such distinctions have no meaning, where the normal guidelines of reality disappear. In "Nocturno de la estatua" (Nocturne of the Statue), one of his best poems, he dreams of a screaming statue which flees his approach. As he rounds a corner after it, he finds only the cry; when he attempts to capture the cry, he finds only the echo, and the effort to seize the echo results only in touching a wall, which in turn becomes an opaque mirror in which he sees only himself. This progression of decreasing concreteness and the confusion of sensory perceptions represent again the ceaseless failure to communicate, the utter isolation into which he has been led by reason and which, at the same time, bursts from his psyche as soon as logical controls are withdrawn. Waking or sleeping, each thing to which he turns disappears, and he finds only himself, the eternal and unique companion. When, at last, he finds the statue—assassinated—and gives it life by closing his eyes (for only in dreams can he hope to achieve his goal), she says to him, "I am dead tired."[68] This deliberate use of a popular cliché underlines the grotesque failure; even this dream companion is dying of the fatal malady, sleep. The entire poem is represented in terms of a nightmare, of a voyage to hell, and sleep becomes both the medium of the search and the irremissible moment of total failure. It is for this reason that Villaurrutia called sleep "a daily provisional death . . .";[69] as we shall see, it is also closely linked with the second of the obsessive themes, the constant presence of death.

But these poems are not merely the record of a repeated nightmare; in wakefulness and sleep, and even in that timeless moment before sleeping, the moment which is neither sleep nor waking, the restless intellect sought the answers to the unanswerable questions. In *"Nocturno en que nada se oye"* (Nocturne in Which Nothing Is Heard), pure intellect, disembodied, records its thoughts in that instant when consciousness has abandoned the body, that "bloodless statue,"[70] to descend interminably, into the water which does not moisten, into the vitreous air, into the livid fire: metaphors of the movement of the mind through that realm where all its frighteningly familiar, yet terribly changed.

In this hallucinated world unspeakable terror lurks at every corner. *"Nocturno sueño"* (Dream Nocturne), suddenly, horribly, but only indirectly, the disembodied intellect meets its own body. In this tangential quality of the encounter resides the greatest horror, for whatever the consequences of coming face to face with one's self, it is at least a direct confrontation. Even this is forbidden: the poet hears the sounds of his own steps as they pass. Suddenly, inexplicably, after the fashion of dreams, he holds a dagger.

> Without a drop of blood
> without sound or weight
> at my frozen feet
> my body fell.
>
> I took it in my arms
> I bore it to my bed.
>
> Sleep closed
> its profound wings.[71]

Physical and intellectual have met again, and once more the search has ended, temporarily, to be renewed in an incessant cycle.

Thus far, we have been concerned primarily with the first of Villaurrutia's obsessive themes, the anguish of absolute personal uniqueness and all that this uniqueness implies. The second major theme, which we encounter first in "Dream Nocturne" and which plays an increasingly important role thereafter, is the implacable presence of death.

In *"Nocturno muerto"* (Dead Nocturne), Villaurrutia describes
with almost affectionate care each detail of the death which
haunts him, from the first slow, tepid breath which will cling
to him like the bandage to the wound to the final opaque solitude
and ashen shadow. Although the emphasis here lies rather on
the moment of death itself than on its previous presence, this
is almost a hymn to death, which is awaited, if not with rejoicing,
certainly with trembling and expectation. In this sense, it is
clearly in the vein of "Death in Tenths." *"Nocturno en que habla
la muerte"* (Nocturne in Which Death Speaks), written in 1935
while Villaurrutia was studying at the Yale Drama School, is
the first clear statement of the concept of individual death which
haunts the later poems, although, as we have seen, it has a
direct antecedent in "Poetry," written eight years earlier. Death
is not here an abstract concept, nor is it the physical fact presented in "Dead Nocturne"; instead, it is an almost concrete
entity, which is the poet's alone. The first stanza, of thirty-five
lines, really consists of two parts. The first is the voice of the
poet as he reflects on the possibility of a *personal* death having
accompanied him, not mentally or spiritually, but like a stow-
away, "hidden in an empty spot of my clothing in the suitcase,/
in the pocket of one of my suits,/ between the pages of a book.
. . ."[72] In the second part, he imagines the words of the personalized Death as she might speak to him:

> . . . Here I am.
> I have followed you like the shadow
> which it is impossible to leave behind at home;
> like a bit of air, calid and invisible
> mixed with the hard cold air you breathe;
> like the memory of what you most love. . . .[73]

Death is strangely near to being the beloved here, "what you
most love. . . ." But this beloved is far more persistent than any
mortal woman, for the sea across which he fled is nothing, nor
is the "dream in which you would like to believe you live/
without me, when I myself sketch it and erase it. . . ."[74] Almost
tenderly, she concludes: "Here I am, don't you feel me?/ Open
your eyes; close them, if you wish."[75] And in the last two brief
verses, the poet is suddenly certain that she has come; a door

closes in an empty room; a paper falls with no breeze to move it; there is a strange pulsation in his pen, and the words which are written are not his own.

This highly personal concept of Death as the inseparable companion, with its ambiguous love-fear attitude, is far from simple fear of the physical fact of dying or the Romantic despair before the extinguishing of the unique individual. Elías Nandino has suggested that death signified for Villaurrutia a return to the essence of the cosmos;[76] such a concept, however, seems much more true of Nandino's own work than of his friend. Rodolfo Usigli feels that it was rather the only stable reality in a world which was rapidly losing its sanity: "the return to death as to a piece of land, the only nontransferable, untouchable, inalienable. . . ."[77] Villaurrutia himself commented directly on his attitude toward death on several occasions, and these remarks underline both the immediacy and the ambiguity of his attitude.

Modern man dies and attends—at least I attend—his own death. And . . . that of the rest. The *memento mori* and the *art of dying* are for me of an anguished immediacy.[78]

Death is, for me, neither an end nor a bridge stretching toward another life, but a constant presence, a living and touching it second by second . . . a presence which surprises in pleasure and in pain.[79]

Death is not, for me, only the end of life. Living to prepare for dying well or simply dying seem to me truths from which one more profound truth remains justifiably absent. Neither am I satisfied to consider life as a prison which we leave, at last, thanks to death. My poetry is the presence of death throughout all of life, since man lives his own death.[80]

. . . At moments like those we now live, death is the only thing which cannot be taken from man; they can take away time, life, illusion, but death, who will take it from me? We carry death, as a poet said, within, as the fruit bears the seed. It accompanies us always, from birth, and our death grows with us. Death is also a fatherland to which one returns; that is why it is possible to have a book of verses called *Nostalgia of Death*. Nostalgia of what is already known. Death is something already known by man.[81]

These flat rejections of death as the end, whether from the
religious or the nihilistic points of view, place Villaurrutia directly in the context of his clearly existential attitude. This in
no way implies that he was a disciple of any particular existentialist philosopher—indeed, as we shall see, there are rather
good grounds to believe that such is not at all the case—or that
he received this concept of death from any one source. The
search for influences on Villaurrutia's development of his theme
has been badly overdone, and later we will attempt to show
that he is well within his own national poetic tradition. He was
an existentialist in the same sense that Antonio Machado,
Quevedo, and many others are existentialists: they are preoccupied by the relationship of life to death as an organic part
of the existential process in its fundamental sense, the process
of existence.

Nostalgia of Death concludes with five poems grouped under
the heading, "Nostalgias"; of these, all with the exception of
"Death in Tenths" appeared in final form in the 1938 edition.
"North Carolina Blues" seems strangely out of place; dedicated
to Langston Hughes, it is an unfruitful effort to assimilate
Hughes's jazz-influenced rhythms and is interesting only because
of several unusually sensual images and Villaurrutia's concise
comment on Jim Crowism.

> In different waiting rooms
> awaiting the same death
> the passengers of color
> and the whites, first-class.[82]

In the three "Nostalgias" properly speaking, Villaurrutia makes
use of the explicit symbol, equating winter and snow directly
to his own spiritual climate. *"Nostalgia de la nieve"* (Nostalgia
of the Snow) is for Villaurrutia, a rare example of the emotional refusal to face the logical consequences of his poetic
single-mindedness. There is a passionate yearning to return to
a time when sleep did not mean a descent into a very personal
hell, a heightening of the very faculties which make the day
torture.

> . . . something of sweet sleep,
> of sleep without anguish,
> childlike, tender, light
> joy unremembered. . . .[83]

"*Cementerio en la nieve*" (Cemetery in the Snow) presents the comparison of a snow-covered cemetery with a corpse, even a corpse twice dead; the falling of the snow upon the cemetery is like the "fall of one silence upon another and of the white persistence of forgetfulness . . .,"[84] like the silence of death falling upon the death-in-life which is the fate of man, condemned to think. However, the best of these poems by far is "*Muerte en el frío*" (Death in the Cold), which closely resembles the first of the nocturnes with its four parallel introductory lines:[85]

> When I have lost all faith in miracle . . .
>
> . . . when the winter sky is no more than the ash
> of something which burned many, many centuries ago . . .
>
> . . . when I find myself so alone, so alone . . .
>
> . . . when I close my eyes thinking uselessly . . .[86]

The torture he suffers is "the cold hell . . . the eternal winter,"[87] another effective use of paronomasia in the yoking of hell-winter (*infierno-invierno*). In this bitter climate of the soul, the poet traces his inevitable fate in a spare style which progresses from setting of mood through despair to an almost stoic contemplation. The heightened perception of this moment of esthetic and intellectual concentration is reflected in a striking series of images:

> . . . I find myself so alone, so alone,
> that I search for myself in my room,
> as one searches, at times, for a lost object,
> a letter crumpled in the corner. . . .[88]

In a stanza strikingly similar to some of the best of Neruda and Quevedo, perhaps the two greatest poets of death in Spanish, he sums up his anguish before the ineluctable fact.

I feel that I am living here my death,
my only present death,
my death which I cannot share or weep,
my death of which I shall never be consoled.[89]

In the last stanza, this intensely personal sense of loss gives way before an almost detached contemplation of the army of infinitesimal workers ceaselessly hammering on the "trembling lymph and flesh. . . ."[90]

. . . how the water and the blood
are once more the same marine water,
and how first it freezes
and then becomes glass
and then hard marble
until I am immobilized in the most anguished, slowest time
with the secret life, mute and imperceptible
of the mineral, of the trunk, of the statue.[91]

Here, perhaps, is the true key to Villaurrutia's concrete imagery, to his use of adjectives which denote opaqueness and hardness, in this final moment when the body returns to the mineral of the earth.

"Death in Tenths" is an intense and ironic summing up, as though death and anguish had become such familiar figures that there was no longer any need for formality. It appeared in the 1938 edition of *Nostalgia of Death* as a sequence of five *décimas,* a verse form composed of ten lines of eight syllables each, with a normal rhyme scheme of *abbaaccddc;* the five in the 1938 edition appear as numbers 3, 4, 5, 6, and 10 of the definitive version, first published in 1941. Villaurrutia said of them, "I wrote the five remaining after a long and involuntary pause."[92] Formally, it is a sequence patterned on the sonnet sequence familiar to the Eliazabethans and uses many of the conventions common to the sequence; the theme is again that of the personal and private death, expressed here on the double level of death the fact, and Death personalized. Thus, the ten *décimas* present a double emotional-intellectual complex, the poet's reaction to his own imminent and inevitable death and simultaneously, an allegory of Death as the Beloved.

The first stanza is a baroque meditation on the nature of his love in a series of linked antithetical constructions. This beloved, however, is no mere woman stooping to momentary folly, but the personification of death, not merely an intellectual concept or a physical fact, but an individual being who awakens in the poet a deep emotional reaction. At the same time, the obsession with solipsism returns in a brilliant parody of Descartes' *Cogito ergo sum;* the constant opposition between life and death is resolved in the substitution of *muero,* I die, for *cogito,* I think. The only proof of our existence is that it must cease to exist, and death, then, is our very being. In an ambivalence which lies behind much of Villaurrutia's poetry, he awaits death not without fear, but expectantly, even eagerly.

The second stanza is again parodic, this time of the Baroque technique which has been called "dispersion and recollection," the summary in the final verse of related elements scattered throughout the poem.[93] Here, this technique and the specific vocabulary of the stanza deliberately recall a number of Baroque sonnets, particularly Góngora's *"Mientras por competir con tu cabello"* (While to Rival Your Hair), with its final verse, "in earth, in dust, in smoke, in shadow, in nothing,"[94] and Sor Juana's *"Este que ves, engaño colorido"* (This You See, Colorful Deceit), with its summary, "is corpse, is dust, is shadow, is nothing."[95] This is hardly coincidental; these two magnificent poems are akin in their profound understanding of the relationship between life and death, and "Death in Tenths" is of the same family. At the same time, Villaurrutia's use of the four elements water-fire-dust-wind recalls Empedocles' four vital principles. They are equivalent to death, which is, then, the sovereign principle. Life is death, and to live is to die.

The third *décima* continues this semiparodic allusive mode; here, the source is the popular verse used by Lope de Vega and Saint Teresa, the famous "Come death so hidden/ that I do not feel you come."[96] The poet hopes that when Death arrives she will do so silently; he is willing and perhaps even eager to see her, but he would prefer the visit to be quiet and without advance notice. This is, of course, also a stock technique of the Elizabethan sonneteer, who often hoped for the same surprise visit in order to savor more fully the joy of the moment, and we see again Villaurrutia's significant use of what is es-

sentially an erotic form to express his attitude toward death.
The fourth stanza is again allusive in that it employs erotic
imagery to express the union with death, just as Renaissance
mystical poetry employed the same sort of imagery to express
the union with God. This inversion of "poesía a lo divino" reflects the shift from the ironic, intellectual mode of the first
verse to the total desire to take part in the final consummation,
which is, in its own way, as much a mystical experience as
the union with God, since for both Villaurrutia and the mystics,
this union signified the ultimate experience, the perception of
the final significance.

In the fifth stanza, Villaurrutia makes extended use of
synesthesia, one of the most effective devices in the creation
of this highly personalized phantomworld, to contrast strikingly
the attributes of this fair lady without mercy, to those of the
less striking, if less fatal, charms of the more orthodox mistress.
Just as the Baroque structure is striking in its unexpectedness,
so the reader is startled to find the mistress referred to as
"your rigid body."[97] She becomes the incarnation of the principle
of death, the principle before which love and life are erased.
In the following stanza, Villaurrutia explores the temporal
significance of this encounter, this fatal embrace beyond space
and time, so far beyond all previous experience that it may even
transcend its own limitations and, paradoxically, create a new
zone of existence in which "it will be possible, perhaps,/ to
live after having died."[98] This contrasts sharply with the return
to erotic imagery in the seventh *décima*, which, while apparently
describing the emotional impact of the sexual act, is actually
anticipating the moment of death. In this parallel, the role of
death becomes clear once more; from the cold dread induced
by the first thought of her, through the agonized metaphysical
speculation, to the longing which her constant presence has
finally produced, she has emerged, not as abstraction, but as
Death. She is no longer a metaphor; she is an enticing mistress.
Thus, the eighth verse is a love poem to an absent mistress,
that is to Death, *the* ultimate beloved. There is no nocturnal
horror as the poet speaks of the extent to which she permeates
his consciousness; he has abandoned such facile reactions for a
more complex understanding. They are linked so indissolubly

that even in her absence "I find you in the hollow/ of a
form. . . ."[99]
But if Death is this personal and unique,

> what will be of you, Death
> when, as I leave the world,
> with the profound knot untied,
> you must abandon me?[100]

With this mocking challenge, Villaurrutia arrives at the final
stanza. There is no fear of the beloved's arrival; in vain Death
may menace him, for he has triumphed. In a concentration
of bitter irony, he shows us again the true nature of this
beloved and taunts her with the knowledge that he has already
violated the hour of their meeting. In an existence whose only
reality is death, "there is no hour in which I do not die!"[101]

"Death in Tenths" is one of Villaurrutia's finest poetic achieve-
ments in its purification of technique and the reduction of
nonessentials in this very personal mode of expression. His
rendezvous with Death and his willingness to recognize the
need to abandon any thought of love as a mode of escape are
a tribute to the personal and poetic integrity which he brought
to the expression of his anguish.

IV *Style and Technique in* Nostalgia of Death

A number of critics have commented on Villaurrutia's predilection for visual and particularly tactual metaphors, to the
point that Jorge Cuesta stated "The plasticity of his poetry is
best adjusted to the equilibrium of forms, to the outline of
objects, to the quality of the material employed, to the static
nature of attitudes";[102] and, "poetry constructed in function of
touch and sight."[103] The reader will recognize the truth of
these statements; Villaurrutia's poetic vocabulary is composed
predominantly of visual and tactual expressions. Further, certain key words are employed repeatedly: night, shadow, solitude,
cold. What is perhaps unusual about *Nostalgia of Death* is the
insistence with which the metaphoric vocabulary and the poetic
technique are subordinated to this same insistence on the immediate, the concrete, or, to use one of Villaurrutia's favorite

adjectives, the opaque nature of reality, as though the poet
were almost able to glimpse the truth beyond the forms which
pursued him.

There are two major aspects of this emphasis which deserve
further comment: personification of the inanimate or abstract,
and use of adjectives whose primary characteristic is their de-
notation of hardness. The former is almost constant: night
"sketches with her hand/ of shadow . . .,"[104] statues flee constantly through streets peopled by the harsh sound of silence,
and so on. Death is a person who is able to secrete herself "in
an empty spot of my clothing in the suitcase,/ in the pocket
of one of my suits,/ between the pages of a book. . . ."[105] Silence
and solitude are repeatedly referred to as "hard," *duro,* and
even the lover's silence becomes "your silence hard crystal of
hard rock. . . ."[106] Repeatedly, the poet's body becomes a frozen
statue, alien to him, encountered at random or turning a corner.
The function of these techniques seems clear; within the hallucinated world of his nocturnal search, the poet is besieged by the
menace of death, not an abstract death but a specific and concrete threat. At the same time, his flight is persistently ob-
structed by objects, which prevent the human communication
which is the only hope for escape. The progressive decorporaliza-
tion in "Nocturne of the Statue" represents the fleeting nature of
human contact, which ends, fatally and irrevocably, in the wall-
mirror, the limits of human personality which prevent any meaningful human relationships. Totally enclosed by the hermetic
oneness, besieged by death, the poet stumbles from one object
to another, groping hopelessly for the touch of another hand in
the "submerged city"[107] in a night which is "the sea of an ancient
dream,/ of a cold and empty dream in which there now remains/
of the sea only the remains of a shipwreck of forgetfulness"
("Nocturne").[108]

One of Villaurrutia's favorite technical devices has awakened
frequent criticism because it has been misunderstood as simple
playing with words, verbal and aural trickery. César Rodríguez
Chicharro has carefully examined it in his "Disemia y paronomasia en la poesía de Xavier Villaurrutia"[109] and finds that the
commonest forms of this device are disemia, double meaning
of the same sound pattern, and paronomasia, use of words con-
taining similar and different phonemes, or, more simply, the

similarity of sounds between the words. It is curious that this device in Villaurrutia should awaken such antipathy, since it is really one of the commonest manifestations of the baroque school of conceptism, the yoking of opposites to achieve paradoxical expression. Given Villaurrutia's well-known preference for Sor Juana Inés de la Cruz, who used such expressions extensively, and the use of the equally baroque quotation from Drayton, there seems no cause for surprise. Villaurrutia is, as Rodríguez Chicharro has pointed out, essentially a neobaroque poet. In addition to the systematic use of such ironic twists in "Death in Tenths," Villaurrutia's poetry abounds in typically baroque antithetical expressions; curiously, these do not seem to have awakened any serious objection, although Arturo Torres Ríoseco refers to marble coldness and affirms that "a pallid smile of death plays on the poet's lips."[110] This seems a misunderstanding of the poet's attitude, and certainly Tomás Segovia is closer to the truth when he affirms that Villaurrutia is the most emotional of the "Contemporáneos" in his poetry.[111] There is no question of coldness, but rather of the need for a restrained ironic mode to control the volcanic theme which strained constantly against form.

In any case, it is not the baroque antithesis but rather the equally baroque use of identical or similar sound patterns with different meanings which has awakened opposition. The harshest criticism is reserved for lines such as the following, from "Nocturne in Which Nothing Is Heard":

> ... y mi voz que madura
> y mi voz quemadura
> y mi bosque madura
> y mi voz quema dura. ...

These four lines are pronounced identically, although they mean four quite distinct things: "And my voice which matures,/ and my burning voice,/ and my mature forest,/ and my voice burns hard. . . ." Nor is this the only poem in which such phonetic trickery plays a major part; others are "Eternal Nocturne" and even the early "Poetry." In his *Ensayos sobre literatura latinoamericana,* Torres Ríoseco refers to these lines as "exercises which, although ingenious, deprive the poem of intensity. . . ."[112]

To represent these lines as simple word juggling is a serious misreading. Villaurrutia himself has commented on this: "I would never put in my poetry a single word without an exact sense or which was purely decorative. If I have used 'word games' it is because they have been necessary to express an idea. Furthermore, the 'word game' appears in Spanish poetry—in Lope, for example—although not with the frequency with which it exists in French poetry, and in English, where it is entirely common."[113] José Luis Martínez has explained their significance in a brilliant elucidation. He refers back to a previous line, "And in the anguished play of one mirror before another/ my voice falls . . .,"[114] and calls this "a graphic and subtle means for representing the anguished rebounding of a voice fallen between the mutual and infinite reflection of two mirrors face to face, reproduced again and again, in their surface, in different tints represented by the play of the words which preserve identical phonemes."[115] These verses seem clearly to be an effort to reproduce the illusion of hearing one's own voice echo and re-echo precisely at the moment of losing consciousness, a phenomenon known to those who have been anesthetized. The same technique is employed a few lines later; the pertinent words are underlined:

> . . . here in the ear's shell
> the beating of a sea in which *I know nothing*
> in which *one does not swim*. . . .[116]

The poet hears the beating of his blood, a reference, of course, to the well-known children's game of listening to the sea in a seashell, which has the same general shape as the human ear. He interprets it as the beating of the sea, of which he knows nothing, for it is produced at the exact moment of losing consciousness, and is, furthermore, the very essence of his existence, the problem which he is attempting to solve. It is a sea in which one dare not swim, for it is a deadly sea which will be heard again when this daily provisional death is exchanged for the final and unique annihilation of consciousness. It has not, perhaps, been widely noted that the title of the poem is exactly the same sort of double meaning. Nothing is heard in both senses; all is silent, but the *nada*, ultimate nothingness personified, speaks clearly.

V   Song to Spring: *The Last Poems*

Villaurrutia's last collection, *Song to Spring and Other Poems*, was published in 1948; it includes the title poem, which won first prize at the Mexico City Spring Festival in 1948, and nine others, several of which had previously appeared elsewhere. This last volume differs considerably from the poet's earlier work; most of the poems are love lyrics, although they are far from the conventional. The beloved is no longer death, but a mortal being, and the anguish of approaching annihilation is replaced by the despair of the disappointed lover. The change of emphasis is not quite crystallized, as though the poet's death had truncated the development of this new tendency. Just as "Death in Tenths" first appeared in unfinished form, "Décimas of Our Love," the best poem in *Song to Spring*, was later published in a revised and incomparably better version. This would indicate that the period represented by the volume may never have attained its final expression.

All this hardly means that the volume is a failure. If it is less successful than *Nostalgia of Death*, the latter sustains a poetic tension not often achieved. The title poem is, despite its name, a hymn to despair. There are reminiscences of the adjectivization of the nocturnes, but there is considerably less of the striking imagery associated with the earlier poems. The first six stanzas represent the arrival of spring; it is a wave, a cloud appearing in the sky, the dream of earth. The second section is composed of four verses which present mankind's reaction. These two sections are particularly atypical in manner and content; they are also rather undistinguished. Even allowing for the possibility of deliberately pedestrian language for purpose of later contrast, such lines as "Because Spring Is a Cloud!" are a distinct shock in a poet whose detestation of stock imagery was well known.

The third section reveals the falsity of this ideal of regeneration, and we see spring in its true nature.

> The smile of the child
> who does not understand the world
> and finds it beautiful:
> of the child who does not yet know![117]

Spring is the whispered promise which awakens eyes and lips, the trembling hope which displaces anguish. What matter if the promise go unfulfilled, if the hope only postpone the inevitable disillusionment, for spring, *primavera,* is above all the first truth, the *primera verdad,* the transitory nature of man's happiness, which seems that it will endure forever and vanishes suddenly, "leaving no more trace/ than that left by the wing/ of a bird on the wind."[118] This last section of the poem is both more typical of the author and considerably better poetry. Villaurrutia does not succeed in making the first portion plausible; the bitter twist of his conception of spring's true meaning is more sincere and more convincing as poetry, but it lacks the compressed agony, the concentrated expression which raises *Nostalgia of Death* to such unusual poetic heights.

"Amor condusse noi ad una morte," which Chumacero has called the end of Villaurrutia's most intense period of poetic creativity,[119] was first published in the review *Taller* in 1939 and later included in *Death in Tenths and Other Poems* (1941). Rather than the end of the period of greatest intensity, it would seem rather to mark the beginning of a period of transition during which Villaurrutia was beginning the series of love poems represented by his last volume of poetry, while completing "Death in Tenths" and perfecting the final version of *Nostalgia of Death.* Chumacero also indicates the similarity in theme and tone between "Amor condusse noi ad una morte" and Salvador Novo's *"Amor"* (Love), from his collection *"Espejo"* (Mirror). Whatever influence Novo's poem may have exercised on Villaurrutia, the source of the title is verse 103 of Canto V of Dante's *Inferno;* the speakers are the ill-fated lovers Francesca and Paolo, killed by Francesca's husband and Paolo's brother Gianciotto when he surprised them in an adulterous affair. Dante's verse refers, of course, to both a physical and a spiritual death, their murder and subsequent damnation, while Villaurrutia's poem refers to the spiritual death of erotic despair, the mood of doubt about the beloved's faithfulness which sets the tone for most of the book. This beloved is not Death, but a living human who maintains the poet in a state of tormented suspense. The expression of this suspense is far more felicitous than the preceding poem; his love is "an anguish, a question,/ a suspenseful and luminous doubt."[120] He is totally absorbed by the beloved, anxious to learn every detail, and yet fearful of knowing.

> Love is the reconstruction, when you are far,
> of your steps, your silences, your words,
> and trying to follow your thought
> when at my side, at last immobile, you are silent.[121]

The mood and imagery are familiar, but the difference is un-mistakable. What had been the effort to establish contact, to penetrate the shell of individuality, is now a lover's anxious effort to possess the beloved completely, mentally and spiritually as well as physically. And even here, he fails.

> Love is not sleeping when in my bed
> you dream between my arms which gird you,
> and hating the dream in which, beneath your forehead,
> perhaps in other arms you are abandoned.[122]

The cast of characters is the same, but the tragedy is now on a poetically lower level, if a more human one. Excellent poetry indeed, but it pales beside the hallucinated agony of the "Nocturnes."

This thirst for total possession of the beloved reappears in "*Soneto de la granada*" (Sonnet of the Pomegranate), with a note of desperate hope that he may find another to share this thirst and, in sharing, to slake it. This is almost a return to the despairing solipsism of the earlier poems; less anguished, perhaps, but equally powerful in its half-believed hope. The imagery marks an almost complete return; his flesh is again hard and cold in its isolation. "*Soneto de la esperanza*" (Sonnet of Hope) is in the same vein, analyzing love in terms of the lover's suffering as he awaits the beloved. His uncertainty drives him to the wish that he might change the nature of their love, captivating her with his thought alone.

The high point of this stage of Villaurrutia's poetry is found in the two poems "*Nuestro amor*" (Our Love) and "*Décimas de nuestro amor*" *(Décimas of Our Love)*. The former is an ef-fort to express the physical and psychological bases of love, but this is hardly an idyll. Love, for Villaurrutia, was a total absorption, including every instant, every mental and physical

phenomenon. Where in *Nostalgia of Death* love had been more
a means of human contact than a state in itself, it is here of
immediate significance, based not on happiness or even, apparently, a profound mutual attraction, but on a mutual anguish,
as though at last, Villaurrutia had found one person capable of
comprehending; it is almost a mutual effort at self-preservation.

> . . . if our love were not
> like a tight thread
> on which we go, we two
> without a net above the abyss. . . .[123]

By its nature, this love is far more important than an ordinary
affair; the lovers are united much more closely by their mutual
agony than they could be by a mutual attraction. If their love
were not this, if it were not a total fusion of this mutual despair,
it could not be.

The three *décimas* included in *Song to Spring* are actually
stanzas 2, 3, and 10 of "Décimas of Our Love," which was published posthumously; it is one of the high points of this period
and indicates a return to the manner of the "Nocturnes." Here
is the same opaque compression of language, the same rigorous
economy which is one of Villaurrutia's most effective qualities,
but applied to the new theme. The anguish of these *décimas*
springs not from contemplation of a death which, however personal, is not the here and now, but from a profound sentiment of
bitter loss. The imagery has not changed; there is the same
insistence on concrete metaphor.

> . . . the somber
> cavern of my agony. . . .[124]

> . . . and when alone I invoke you,
> in the dark stone I touch
> your impassible company.[125]

> My love for you did not die,
> it goes on living in the cold,
> unknown gallery
> which it dug in my heart.[126]

There are the same baroque reminiscences of contrast and antithesis.

> For the fear of loving me
> as much as I love you,
> you have preferred, rather,
> to save yourself, losing me.[127]

There is a return to the despair of *Nostalgia of Death,* a return to the desolation of the knowledge of the utter vacuity of existence.

> . . . why do we not break
> this painful and withered anguish
> to leave this nothingness?[128]

> . . . I hear your voice in the echo
> and I find your form in the emptiness
> which you have left in the vacuum.[129]

These verses, identical in tone and style with the best of the nocturnes, can only cause us to ask whether Villaurrutia would not perhaps have returned to the spirit of his earlier work, or whether he would have gone on in the new direction indicated in the bulk of *Song to Spring.*

The remaining poems are of minor importance. *"Inventar la verdad"* (To Invent the Truth) is a conventional love lyric, interesting only because of the transformation of conventional diction by Villaurrutian imagery. *"Madrigal sombrío"* (Somber Madrigal) might almost be another stanza of "Our Love," although lacking some of the latter's impact.

Included in this section in the complete works are several poems which did not appear in the 1948 edition. *"Deseo"* (Desire) and *"Palabra"* (Word) were written at some point before 1938 but were first published in 1953.[130] Curiously, "Desire" is a love poem close to the idiom of "Our Love" and demonstrates that even as early as the first edition of *Nostalgia of Death,* Villaurrutia was experimenting in the new direction, while "Word" is a brief four-line stanza of no real significance. "Mar" (Sea) was published at the same time, but in the second edition of the works is included among the early poems, although in tone it is far closer to later works. It treats the sea as though it were human, a lover to be held tightly lest it, too, escape. This is an unusual poem in that it is one of the rare instances in which water retains for Villaurrutia its traditional symbolic significance of love and regeneration even here, and expectedly,

> . . . although I was yours, cold between your arms,
> your heat and your breath were in vain:
> I feel you ever less mine.[131]

The "*Soneto del temor a Dios*" (Sonnet of the Fear of God) was first published in 1950; it is a highly unusual work for Villaurrutia. If it were not for the title, the sonnet could well be another in the sequence of desolate love poems which preoccupied him at the time of his death, with an echo of the ambiguous attitude toward the beloved seen in "Death in Tenths." It is, however, possible to interpret the unnamed "you" of the poem as God, in view of the title, which would then cause us to read the sonnet as an effort to find some religious understanding and the failure of this attempt. It is also conceivable that the "Fear of God" of the title refers ironically to the poet's frustration at his inability to snare the beloved in his net of words. Whether God or the beloved—and, given Villaurrutia's motion of love, there is no real reason to discard the double intention—he is helpless.

> My fever to reach you is useless,
> while you who can do all
> do not come to be ensnared in my net.[132]

"*Epigramas de Boston*" (Boston Epigrams), published in 1949 in the review *Prometeus*, is a series of light ironic comments on a Boston which is both traditional and stylized, the Boston of George Apley, the Lowells, and the cod. Neither intent nor import is substantial.

Three further poems not included in the original edition (and in two cases, unpublished in book form) deserve rather more extended comment. "*Cuando la tarde . . .*" (When the Evening . . .) was found among Villaurrutia's papers at his death and was included by Chumacero in the section *Nostalgia of Death* of the collected works. The poem bears substantial similarities of style and vocabulary to the poems of this book, but its theme makes this attribution dubious. The basic metaphor of the poem is that of the dusty, ashen city from whose every cranny night creeps. However, it ends startlingly (for Villaurrutia) in that this lurking night brings, not the livid nightmare of always, but, simply, desire. The development of the poem is such that the reader anticipates the fatal slip into the renewed nightly small death, and the final climactic word is both unexpected and jarring. Given the return toward the end of Villaurrutia's life to the idiom of *Nostalgia of Death* for the expression of a theme which, if not precisely erotic, is rather closely allied, "When the Evening . . ." would seem rather to belong to the sequence represented by *Song of Spring* than to the earlier poems.

"Estatua" (Statue) was first published in the review *Los Sesenta* in 1963; its date of composition appears to be unknown. The poem is curious in that it describes a supposed statue, or more likely, an unnamed person who has succeeded in forging an impenetrable wall about himself, such that he is isolated from all others, finally and perfectly. The vocabulary is certainly that of the best nocturnes, but the sense of final acceptance, of resignation before the ultimate knowledge of absolute and irredeemable solitude, suggest that "Statue" may well have been a late poem, a step—perhaps the last?—in the swing back to the themes of *Nostalgia of Death*. This possibility is reinforced by Villaurrutia's last poem, *"Volver"* (Return), written just a few hours before his death and given to his close friend and physician, Elías Nandino; it was unpublished until 1960. "Return" is a compact expression of what must surely have preoccupied the poet during his last hours, particularly in view of Nandino's statement to this writer that he had shortly before warned Villaurrutia that he had a cardiac disturbance and that he should exercise caution. Instead, the poet attended a party at which he was his typical witty self, enjoyed himself enormously, danced extensively, and returned home to die. The poem is quite brief.

> Return to a distant fatherland,
> return to a forgotten fatherland,
> obscurely deformed

by the exile in this land.
To leave the air which encloses me!
And anchor once again in the nothing.
The night is my mother and my sister,
the nothing is my distant land,
the nothing full of silence,
the nothing full of emptiness,
the nothing without time or cold,
the nothing in which nothing happens.[133]

This is certainly an extraordinary poem to have been written at that particular time under those particular conditions, although its signifiance in the poet's final hours can be only conjectured. In any case, the theme, the vocabulary, and even the totally typical verbal play between *destierro-tierra* (exile-land) and the two meanings of *nada*, "nothing," in the last line, place this poem squarely in the line of *Nostalgia of Death*. Even further, this is virtually a poetic statement of the theme of Villaurrutia's adaptation of *Hamlet, Invitation to Death*, written a number of years earlier, and it clearly suggests that the phase of *Song to Spring* was transitory and that the last few years of creation mark a gradual return to the expression of the obsessive themes of solitude and death.

Song to Spring concludes with two brief "Epitaphs," the first of which is dedicated to J. C., almost certainly Jorge Cuesta, since it is virtually a definition of Cuesta's life and death. The second bears no identifying initials. It is perhaps not overly romantic a temptation to see in it Villaurrutia's own farewell.

Here sleeps, silent and unknown,
one who in life lived a thousand and one deaths.
Do not wish to know of my past.
Awakening is dying. Do not wake me![134]

CHAPTER 3

The Theater

During the later years of Villaurrutia's life, the theater played an increasingly important role, and the total of his dramatic writings is quantitatively far greater than that of his poetry. Nevertheless, the distinction sometimes drawn between the poet and the playwright seems to us false, and the themes underlying the dramas are organically related to those in which the poems are rooted. Behind the experimentalism of the one-act plays, obscured by the apparent commercial conformity of the longer works, and obvious in the remarkable *Invitación a la muerte* (Invitation to Death) are the same implacable search for significance and the same stripping away of nonessentials which produced the dynamic compression of the best poems.

I Autos Profanos: *The Experimental Period*

During the early years of *Ulises* and *Orientación,* Villaurrutia restricted his activities in the theater to directing and translating. It was not until 1933, the fifth season of the experimental movement, that his first original play was staged under the direction of Celestino Gorostiza, the one-act *Parece mentira* (Incredible).[1] It was followed the next years by *¿En qué piensas?* (What Are You Thinking About?); these two form part of a group of five one-acters written during the same period and published in 1943 under the collective title *Autos profanos.* The title is deceptively difficult to translate, since the *Auto* in Spain is a short religious allegory relating to the sacraments, usually communion; although its sources are in the medieval tradition which shows its kinship to the mystery plays, its flowering belongs to the Baroque. It would be totally misleading to pursue too far any intent on Villaurrutia's part to suggest some hidden religious significance to these plays. Rather, he used the term to point out that he, like the authors of the traditional *Autos,*

69

was concerned with certain problems relating to ultimate realities, but his realities lie outside the realm of orthodox religion.
The title, then, is perhaps best translated as *Worldly Mysteries*
or something of the sort.

These plays were written as a conscious measure of self-
discipline, as the author pointed out in his preface.

Difficult because of their apparent simplicity, one-act plays are
equivalent, in a game of comparative rhetorics, to forms as concrete,
sustained and dangerous as the sonnet. There is no better discipline
for a dramatic author than submission to the test of the one-act
play. . . . Perhaps I wrote them for this reason, and, surely, because
of this I have for them a lucid affection.[2]

These *Autos* are, for the most part, high comedy of an experimental nature, aimed at reviving an ossified art. Underlying
the theatrical, however, is a series of obliquely treated intellectual problems; we shall see that this is typical even of the
later more commercial works. Almost all Villaurrutia's dramatic
works display a bifurcation between two different, although
interwoven directions: the conceptual, reflected in a series of
intellectual and even metaphysical problems, and the personal,
in the form of difficult human relationships. Villaurrutia emphasizes this intellectual aspect of his theater in the preface to
Autos profanos; he states that "the audience loves an enigma . . .
it is not necessary to give them a single solution for it, when
one has succeeded in drawing them into the game, intriguing
them, menacing them with the cry of the Sphinx: 'Guess or I
devour you.' "[3] This is certainly an appropriate concept of the
drama for the expression of the problems Villaurrutia wished
to survey, problems which are at the heart of much contemporary
theater, such as the nature of time or the ambivalence of the
personality. If the *Autos* seem at times excessively conceptual,
they are also particularly seductive formulations of these preoccupations. Further, they are, for the most part, highly theatrical, with a considerable proportion of high humor.

Incredible bears the subtitle *Enigma in One Act.* It is set in
the waiting room of an attorney's office, and the characters are,
simply, the Clerk, a Husband, a Curious Man, an Attorney,
and three Ladies. The physical action consists of the successive

entrances and exists of the characters and the reactions of the
three major figures, the Clerk, the Husband, and the Curious
Bystander, particularly in view of the identical actions and words
of the three Ladies who appear to be the same woman.

The Clerk is a fascinating blend of receptionist and poet;
he dominates the scene through his intellectual power as he
expresses the concepts which are the *raison d'être* of the play.
Despite the subtitle, this is not simply a puzzle. An enigma, it is
at the same time an experiment in the dramatic possibilities of
the relative nature of time; the momentary conjunction of different times. The three women who, one after another, enter, speak
the same words, and leave, are the same woman, a condensation
of past time. Three previous visits have been compressed into
the space of a few minutes, as though time were an accordion
to be expanded or compressed.

Along with this preoccupation, *Incredible* explores the
ambivalence of personality. Each character is really an agglomeration of a series of different personalities, reflecting at times
contradictory sentiments, and we catch glimpses of all these,
but only glimpses.

There is an interesting antecedent of modern existentialist
thought in the Clerk's belief that suffering is a necessary part
of existence. The Husband has lived in a false happiness; he
has, he confesses, barely known that he existed. The Clerk's
answer points the way to the only possible decision.

. . . think that the comfort and the ignorance in which your life
developed were no more than an empty reality, an uninhabited world,
a road without a landscape, a sleep without dreams: in a word, a
living death; and that now . . . thanks to a revelation, the revelation
of a secret, you find yourself on the threshold of an existence which
you can debate, correct and shape to your taste. . . .[4]

It is obvious that this notion is related to the concept underlying Villaurrutia's poetry, that of the acceptance of the totality
of individual existence, with all that this implies in terms of
individual suffering. We are most human when we are most
fully aware of our anguish. None of these concepts is fully
developed here; neither the momentary conjunction of tangential
times in which we exist, nor the multifaceted personalities

which we attempt to organize into a coherent whole, nor the acceptance of suffering as a basic aspect of that whole. Villaurrutia's purpose was not to present logical answers to philosophical questions, but to dazzle us with the verbal and conceptual spectacle which makes us reflect on the ultimate mysteries before which we too are only curious bystanders.

What Are You Thinking About?, written and first staged in 1934, is subtitled *Mystery*. Villaurrutia states of it, *"¿En qué piensas?* has, consciously, an appearance of banality, but the parade is inside. I remember that a reviewer accused it of being 'intranscendental,' but in his review he spoke of Bergson, of notions of time, of psychic time. He did not realize that he was putting his finger exactly on the wound. . . ."[5] Here again the theme is the relativity, or perhaps more exactly the personal nature of time, and here, more than in the previous work, it finds expression through some highly complicated interpersonal relationships. The characters are María Luisa, who clearly stands for the Eternal Woman, and the three men who love her, each in his own segment of time. Carlos, Víctor, and Ramón, past, present, and future, are Eternal Man, helpless before this woman who lives, rather than thinks. Ramón exists for her only in function of his confession of his love for her; when she in turn must speak the name of her beloved, she does so by means of what is almost a conjugation of the verb: "I love, simply, I love whoever loves me."[6]

The title, of course, is taken from the eternal lover's question. Maria Luisa invariably answers, "About you," but, unfortunately for the lover in turn, it is obvious that she is not thinking of him at all, and highly dubious that she is capable of thought. This is both a lighthearted comment on the nature of woman and one of the major sources of the play's humor. *What Are You Thinking About?*, better integrated and less uneven than *Incredible*, is both a manifestation of real or psychic time as opposed to false or chronological time, and Villaurrutia's comic homage to the mystery of woman, the eternal female principle before which men are, as Carlos, Víctor, and Ramón learn to their mingled horror and delight, helpless children.

"Ha llegado el momento" (The Moment Has Arrived), and *"El ausente"* (The Absent One), unlike the two preceding plays, deal in a far more realistic fashion with sharply defined personal

crises. The former, written in 1934 and first staged four years
later, takes place at a farewell dinner party; Antonio and Mercedes are about to leave on a mysterious trip. As the dialogue
reveals an increasing uneasiness, a state of tension develops.
Through a series of double-edged references, we finally realize
that the trip is in reality the lovers' double suicide, to which
they have been brought by their sense of estarangement, of loss
of any significance to their relationship.

Mercedes: Antonio and I have looked all over this city, this house,
for something which we have lost. We have sought in every
corner, we have turned on every light. We haven't found it. And
now, by mutual agreement, we are going to look for it in the
only place where we are sure not to find it.[7]

The tension mounts; Mercedes slowly, very slowly, pours her
glass of veronal, and a shot sounds from other room. Then,
relief—Antonio has accidentally fired, and the two lovers realize
with dismay that they have very nearly killed themselves, each
because he or she felt the other no longer loved. The brilliant
tension of the play is resolved in a contrived semi-farcical ending
which is frankly disappointing. Paradoxically, Villaurrutia was
betrayed by the very skill with which he prepared for the surprise ending. Again, the subtitle indicates the tone of the play;
this *Epilogue in One Act* is an epilogue to a love affair, after
the ecstasy and the intoxication of the passions have given way
and there remains only the vacuum left by the lost love.

The Absent One is a far better play, quite possibly the best
of the five. Written in 1937 and not staged until 1951, it deals
with Fernanda's patient wait for her husband Pedro to abandon
the other woman and return home. When this happens, he is
accompanied by the woman, who offers to permit Pedro to
return to Fernanda if the rival too may live with them. Fernanda
is incapable of accepting this *ménage à trois* and prefers to
give up Pedro entirely. She is an extraordinary character in a
carefully constructed play, far stronger than Mercedes or María
Luisa. Villaurrutia's feminine characters tend to be the focal
points of the action, and Fernanda is one of the best. Where
María Luisa dominates the play through the animal magnetism
of a type and Mercedes is both dramatically and morally stronger

than Antonio, if a bit too relentless to be entirely true, Fernanda is more human, alive and passionate than either.

Incredible may well be the most stimulating of the five works and *What Are You Thinking About?* the most theatrical, but *The Absent One* is certainly the most dramatic. Villaurrutia succeeded in raising a tawdry problem to almost mythic stature in this aptly subtitled *Myth in One Act*. Fernanda is faced with the necessity for a moral choice between the myth of Pedro, that is, the memory of Pedro as he was, and the physical consolation of the Pedro who is. Fully conscious of the significance of her choice, she chooses the myth, and as the play ends, she prepares to face a life alone with only this myth of what once was to accompany her. Within the limits of the one-act play, Fernanda becomes very nearly an archetype.

Sea Ud. breve (Be Brief), written in 1934 and never staged, is obvious farce, with overtones of political satire. Its protagonist is the politician Napoleon, who has embarked on a birth control campaign on the assumption that it is perfectly clear that the remedy to illiteracy and joblessness is a sharp decrease in the number of candidates for these categories. His campaign fails totally in the face of the revelation that he is himself the father of a seemingly infinite series of progeny. The farce is only mildly amusing; Napoleon's campaign never achieves the necessary spark, despite some hilarious moments such as the obstinate opposition of the wet nurses' union.

The *Autos profanos*, despite the variations in subject and style, are substantially similar. They are all completely modern in tone and obviously take place in the world of today. All are free of localism of thought, language, or presentation; the themes are valid for all. Perhaps the outstanding common trait, understandably, is their verbalism—the use of dialogue to further mood and action while at the same time providing humor. An example of this takes place in *The Moment Has Arrived*, when Antonio and Mercedes have become so bored with each other that they no longer even quarrel. Mercedes' friend Fernanda sighs that her Luis too refuses to quarrel or even become jealous, and recounts one of her attempts to inflame his jealous interest.

. . . I have tried all the tricks: I talk in my sleep and I confess sins I
haven't committed, I write him anonymous letters telling him that I
am deceiving him, I invite my old sweethearts to dine. One day, when
I saw Luis arriving, I embraced the Japanese chauffeur. . . .[8]

And even as we laugh at Fernanda's semiserious dismay, we
realize that the rift between Antonio and Mercedes is so great
that even such absurd efforts are useless.

Although *What Are You Thinking About?* seems at first situation comedy, what with one lover trying to rid himself of a
jealous former suitor before María Luisa arrives, and the rival's
equally stubborn refusal to leave, the humor of the play is again
largely verbal.

María Luisa: When Carlos loved me, as you do now, you didn't
    know that you loved me already, but I loved you then because
    I knew that one day you would love me.
Carlos *(enraged)*: And now it's Ramón's turn.
María Luisa: You don't understand . . . it's not his turn. None of you
    is later or after another in my love. . . . I love you, not because
    you've stopped loving me, but because you loved me one day.
Víctor: That's fine, but what about me?
María Luisa: I just love you, that's all.
Víctor: But then Ramón is left over.[9]

Rapid verbal humor while it causes audience laughter, darts
rapidly over the fragility of human emotion and leads inevitably
to the final scene of María Luisa surrounded by her helpless,
bemused and confused lovers.

It is this same sort of humor which saves *Be Brief* from total
failure. Perhaps the best example of the theatrical use of this
verbal humor is Napoleon's reaction as he picks up the business
card ostentatiously dropped by the Prostitute. He wavers and
begins to tear it up; then, thinking of his campaign to reduce
the birthrate, mutters, "Let us preach by example."[10] Another
sample is his double-edged commentary on the Young Lady.

Napoleon: . . . it would be well for us to remember that among those
    present there is an unmarried lady.
Young Lady *(ashamed of it)*: I, sir.
Napoleon *(after a rapid examination)*: Yes, just as it should be.[11]

The only work of the five which does not rely largely on this verbal humor is *The Absent One,* where it would have been much too obtrusive. *Incredible,* on the other hand, is composed almost completely of such dialogues; without it, the play does not exist, for the humor is an integral part of the development.

All five plays are simple in setting and stage effects; only in *Be Brief* is the set more than barely outlined. One reason for this simplicity is the fact that at least two, and probably all, were written to be staged in Antonieta Rivas Mercado's salon, where there was insufficient space for elaborate settings. Another factor is the author's intent to direct them himself, as he did on several occasions, and that he was present for the performances and rehearsals of those presented by Orientación. The only real innovation is the emphasis on the use of lighting for dramatic effect, probably under the influence of Gordon Craig. Even this is hardly radical, except in the sense that it is one of the early uses in Mexico of lighting for dramatic effect, and closely related to dramatic progress. The final tableau of *What Are You Thinking About?* is set in a light which suggests the timeless qualities of María Luisa: "Pause. A mysterious overhead light invades the study. All remain immobile, abstracted."[12] This technique is also employed in the other plays: the final scenes of *Incredible* are played in a light which is described as "the opaque light of an aquarium."[13] Napoleon's ideas are signaled by the appearance of "an aureola of sidereal light [which] shines about his head . . .,"[14] and *El ausente* is played against the shadows cast by a small lamp.

As the reader can easily determine, these plays are avant-garde, but hardly spectacularly daring in the context of international theater of the time. They reflect preoccupations of English, French, and Italian drama, and it is sometimes difficult to understand why the work of Villaurrutia and his associates should have aroused such vitriolic personal and artistic enmity. As has been indicated in the first chapter, the antagonism was basically extraliterary; art had a social function, and the artist unwilling to compromise his esthetic integrity by caroling along in the official choir was subject to vilification and sometimes personal and economic reprisals. With the perspective of time, it is obvious that the *Autos profanos* are directly in the tradition of occidental theater; their novelty lies in the fact that they are unlike anything previously attempted in Mexico. In an article written before the composition of the later realistic works, Villaurrutia clarifies his intent:

> The servile, photographic imitation of external models and of fragments of an equally external life have been relegating the theater to a place among the arts which it does not deserve.
>
> The dramatic author forgets, most of the time, that he is an inventor, a creator, a poet; and that the theatrical work has the duty to objectivize and materialize, not what is in fact already objectivized and materialized for the eyes of all, but what is not yet so and which, profound and fleeting, deserves to be so.
>
> Perhaps the road of the contemporary theater is a complete reversal, a radical change of the stage media, to arrive at a profounder capture of the internal and external reality of man.
>
> The theater has its particular poetry: in language, in action, in surprise; in the creation of what we could call the poetry of action. The theater is, among many other things, plastic. But it is not only plastic. It is also architecture and diction, music, dance. The plasticity is only a theatrical means, and should not ever be considered, alone, of itself, an end.[15]

It is interesting to note that, although he never carried this approach to its logical conclusion, Villaurrutia was, theoretically at least, within the mainstream of drama of recent years which has produced the concept of total theater and which has been influential even on professional drama, as seen in works such as *Man of La Mancha* and many others of recent vintage.

II Invitation to Death

As a result of his work in the experimental theater, Villaurrutia was awarded a Rockefeller Foundation grant for study at the Yale Drama School, along with his friend Rodolfo Usigli. For five years after his stay at Yale, he continued to study the theater, to direct and to attempt to crystallize his own dramatic techniques. The only play from this period, and perhaps the only one written during this time, is also his best, the provocative adaptation of *Hamlet, Invitación a la muerte* (Invitation to Death). Written in 1940, it was not produced until 1947, and then passed virtually without comment, almost certainly because it was far too advanced for the Mexican stage of the time.

The play deals with Alberto, owner of a funeral agency, whose father has disappeared a number of years before. Alberto is a strange and tormented figure, unable to establish any meaningful basis of communication with his mother, whom he rightly suspects of an affair, or with his sweetheart Aurelia. His father's return—from voluntary exile?, from the dead?—impels Alberto to break out of his enervating surroundings, but the attempted escape fails; Alberto is unable to function in the world of trains, streets and bustling people. Frustrated and baffled, he returns to sink ever further into the atmosphere of his surroundings and commune ever more closely with death.

The correspondences between *Hamlet* and *Invitation to Death* are obvious: the son's love for his departed father and his resentment of the mother's adulterous affair, the faithful friend, the peculiar attitude toward the sweetheart and the final abandonment of her, the father's ghost, the abortive journey. There are close resemblances to *Hamlet* in the development of certain scenes. Alberto's castigation of his mother's infidelity is similar to Hamlet's; Alberto and his friend Horacio, corresponding to Hamlet and Horatio, both make use of the wall draperies to watch and listen, just as Polonius spied from behind the arras. Alberto, like Hamlet, is paralyzed into inertia and has a nervous collapse; like him, he customarily wears black. Even the names are similar: Hamlet is Alberto, Ophelia becomes Aurelia, Horatio is Horacio, and the action takes place in the sardonically obvious Denmark Funeral Palor.

The idea of a contemporary Hamlet had occurred to Villaurrutia much earlier. In *Queen of Hearts,* Julio, the semiautobiographical hero, visits a funeral home, whose two employees are the obvious sources of the two employees of *Invitation to Death,* who are at the same time, Polonius and Horatio. Speaking of the one who was to become Horacio, he adds, "He makes one think . . . of the gravedigger become mortician whom Shakespeare would put in his *Hamlet* if he were a contemporary of ours."[16]

However, Villaurrutia has done much more than change the locale from Elsinore to Mexico City and the time from the medieval to the present. He has cut or eliminated everything which has no bearing on his reworking of the theme; the gross businessman, equivalent to Claudius, appears for only a brief scene; there seems to be no hint that the father was murdered, if he is indeed dead. The deaths of Polonius, Ophelia, Hamlet, and all the rest are deleted; Laertes does not exist. Only those elements are retained which are pertinent to this story of a modern Hamlet. Thus, the entire focus of the play changes. *Invitation to Death* is not a revenge play; it is not the drama of a tormented, sensitive youth attempting to work his courage to the pitch necessary to kill his stepfather, but of an equally tormented, equally sensitive youth trying desperately to determine his role in the worlds of life and death. It is closely related to the world of the nocturnes, where the ambivalence of personality becomes the anguished solipsism of no longer being what one was, condemned to hear forever more only the sound of one's own voice. In *Invitation to Death,* Villaurrutia has in a sense dramatized *Nostalgia of Death;* he has created an absorbing study of a man's effort to find his own reality.

Alberto is an extraordinarily sensitive youth, grown to maturity in an atmosphere of gloom and preoccupation with death. His days are spent in the funeral home, surrounded by coffins and employees who feel that an air of lugubrious commiseration is the only possible attitude in their profession. The atmosphere at home is no better; the drawing room is decorated in a manner hardly calculated to instill joy into anyone.

. . . Everything seems prepared to provoke espionage. The walls, draped in a slate blue color; the furniture, covered in a dull green, to deaden words rather than to facilitate conversation. A door, rear, leads to Alberto's room; another, left, to the vestibule; two, right, to the library and the living room. More than doors, they are hollows totally disguised by curtains of the same dull green as the furniture, full of folds to disguise the forms. A few more details would make of this anteroom the broadcasting room of a radio station; every object that might provoke an echo has been carefully avoided, and even the light, in the afternoon, when it filters through walls and curtains, seems to express itself in a low voice.[17]

As indicated above, in his development of the Hamlet theme, Villaurrutia has added a good deal of new material. The two long scenes between the two employees have only remote antecedents in Shakespeare's gravediggers; in *Invitation to Death*, these two scenes are of considerable importance in the

setting of mood. Another addition is the veiled woman, rein-
carnation of Juana la Loca (1479-1555), wife of Felipe el
Hermoso and daughter of Ferdinand and Isabella. According to
legend, Juana was driven mad by her husband's marital infideli-
ties and early death, and traveled with his corpse for some
weeks. The veiled woman has sworn to keep the corpse of her
husband with her at all times or wear forever her widow's
weeds. She refuses, of course, to face the only practical solution,
the cremation of her husband. The exact significance of this
scene is difficult to determine; it may be intended to show
Villaurrutia's ironic contempt for rituals over a corpse which
no longer contains the person which once inhabited it; it may
be intended primarily as counterpoint to the obvious lack of
such scruples on the part of Alberto's mother.

The nature of Alberto's problem can be expressed in relatively
simple terms, although these terms are at best verbal approxima-
tions of an extremely complex psychological and emotional
state. Accustomed to his surroundings, desolate over the disappearance of his father, preoccupied at all times with death,
he has reached such a state of dreaming wakefulness that he is
incapable of action. He is unable to escape to another life,
whether it be that offered in another city, or that offered by
his father, who has come to bear him off into the realm of
death. There is no scapegoat for this sacrifice, no surrogate;
Alberto can only dream of the day when he will pass completely
into the world of dreams—or perhaps the absence of them.
Living or dead, he belongs to death.

It is obvious that within the framework of the Hamlet myth,
Villaurrutia is still preoccupied by the themes which dominate
his poetry. Alberto, after his abortive flight, speaks of destiny
and its corollary, death.

And now here, at your side, I understand that it was all as though
my shadow had wanted to abandon forever my body, going out to
seek its destiny, which is not mine . . . because destiny, what we call
destiny, is not outside us, in a city, in a date, in a person, but inside
us, in the very center of us . . . and now I know too that we cannot
leave that destiny, abandoning it, or renouncing it, not even by
seeking death, because then, who is to say that suicide was not precisely our destiny?[18]

This constriction is not a prison. Each person must seek his destiny and abide by it.

. . . I am here in this atmosphere, within these walls, surrounded by this furniture and by these objects which are the image or the company of death, because death is my element, as water is the fishes'. And tell me, who would think that the fish is prisoner in the water? To wish to go out to life, is, in my case, a madness which would drown me. . . .[19]

This is almost identical in tone and theme with the major part of *Nostalgia of Death;* it is, in a sense, and given the tone of resigned acceptance, Villaurrutia's statement of acceptance. Further, Alberto, in one of his best speeches, analyzes his own personality in words which are almost a "Nocturne" in prose form.

I understand that for whole weeks I abandon her to a monotonous, colorless life, in order to follow my own, afraid of breaking the solitude which envelops me. I understand that I am egotistical, cold and hard, at times, like a man of glass; but, like a man of glass, if a foreign breath clouds me, a suspicion, a doubt, they shatter me. Imagine the time I need then to remake myself in a slow, painful scarring, a scarring without blood . . . a lymphatic scarring.[20]

Invitation to Death is, obviously, Villaurrutia's extended dramatic formulation of the same obsessive themes which dominate his poetry. It is, however, something more than this. Giuseppe Bellini, in a penetrating study of *Invitation to Death,* sees it as the representation of modern man, facing multiple problems and incapable equally of finding answers and of ceasing his search.[21] Alberto is, for Bellini, existential man, alienated from his world and his time, disoriented and anguished. The question of Villaurrutia's possible affiliation with existentialism has been raised in connection with his poetry, and although it is more properly studied in connection with possible influences on his work, it is clear that there are considerable affinities between Villaurrutia's conception of existence and that of several existentialist philosophers. It would, however, be erroneous to regard Villaurrutia as a member of such a movement or even as more than a similar spirit finding, largely through his own tormented thought, rather similar answers to closely related questions.

Further, Bellini carefully points out that he regards Alberto as representing the existential anguish of the Mexican and not as a copy of European modes.[22] It seems clear that Villaurrutia is in the European tradition of twentieth-century literature, the tradition of man disoriented and rootless, but he is also within a particular Mexican tradition, as we shall see.

In addition to the metaphysical preoccupation in *Invitation to Death*, there is the beginning of a concentration on interpersonal relationships which becomes increasingly important in the later plays. A major aspect of this is the identification of child with parent. Alberto is virtually a replica of his father, if we can judge from the comments of the other figures, and we shall see this absolute identification again in *The Legitimate Wife*. Another aspect is the insistence on the struggle between child and foster parent. Here, it is Alberto reacting against the lover. It is true that the basic source lies in the Hamlet story, but the same problem is so evident in some later works that this is clearly a fundamental theme of Villaurrutia's theater. A third aspect of this complex of individual relationships is that of the personality which derives sustenance from those who surround it, a major theme in the later *The Ivy* and *The Legitimate Wife*. In *Invitation to Death*, Alberto, without the constant presence of Horacio, slips into an amorphous state of nonbeing. In Alberto, these three themes are focused in one personality. It is this focus which gives such power to the work; it is this personality which dominates the play and makes of it absorbing drama.

Despite the metaphysical tone of much of the play, it is invested with a high degree of theatricality; it is far from being simply a dramatized problem. There is significant use of parallelism in stage setting, in the first and last acts, pointing out the inevitability of Alberto's disaster. During the final moments of the first act, it becomes obvious that Alberto is expecting a visitor. The ambiguity of this unseen visitor and Alberto's collapse lead to his final actions which are, therefore, all the more effective. The repetition of this setting in the final scene, with the addition of the closing of the coffin lid, signaling his final and ultimate surrender to death, provides a remarkable moment.

There is also an interesting and effective episode with the telephone call between the Lover and the Mother, which not only provides some moments of acute suspense, but also a better understanding of Alberto, Horacio, and their relationship. The stage settings are also utilized for maximum dramatic effect; the drawing room has already been mentioned, but an equally effective and provocative setting is the funeral home itself, with an oversized coffin prominently displayed. The possibilities of light and shadow are also utilized. Aurelia is symbolized by light; her first entrance is accompanied by Alberto's turning on a brighter lamp. Alberto, on the contrary, customarily turns down the lights when he enters a room. While he awaits his father, the stage is in complete darkness, and when he rushes outside to find the father he has rejected, the interior lights are dimmed and the outside illumination brightened. The importance of such visual and aural elements are clear in the agonizing tenseness of the final moment.

The agency remains empty. The silence seems to vibrate. The interior light becomes opaque, milky, while the outside lights are intensified. Without anyone or anything moving it, the lid of the coffin in the showcase closes with a brief dry blow. The pause is deeper. Through the glass of the show window we see Alberto return. He is alone. He opens. He enters. The lights have returned to their normal intensity. Alberto breathes deeply. He leaves his hat by his coat. After glancing at the furniture, he arranges two chairs as at the end of the first act. Then, he puts out the main light. The light of the table lamp remains. He sits in the chair at the left. He looks at his watch. He shudders. And then, little by little he becomes still, without turning his head, with his eyes fixed and empty before him, shuddering.
Alberto *(in a low voice, as though to himself):* Is it you, father? Is it you?[23]

III   *The Commercial Theater: 1941-1950*

How much the difficulties of having *Invitation to Death* produced may have influenced Villaurrutia's decision to enter the professional, commercial theater, is uncertain; how strongly the play's failure may have strengthened this conviction, we do not know. However, it is clear that almost at the beginnings of *Ulises*, the eventual intent of the group was the invasion of the commercial stage, and their failure and the opposition of certain

entrenched sectors seems to have delayed the move, but not prevented it. Whatever the reasons, Villaurrutia began in 1941 a
series of realistic, conventionally written and constructed plays
which constitute the major portion of his dramatic output.
Certainly, a major factor was the desire to achieve a larger
public than could have been reached by any continuation of the
small experimental groups with which he had been affiliated.

The first of these plays is *La hiedra* (The Ivy), staged
in 1941, which received a prize from the Cultural and Technical
Council on Entertainment for the best new work of the year.
Written for the actress María Teresa Montoya, it is based on
the theme of Euripides' *Hippolytus,* although Villaurrutia's
treatment is, in its outlines, closer to Racine's version, *Phèdre,*
than it is to the original. Basically, the plot consists of the
growing semi-incestuous love between Hipólito and his widowed
stepmother, Teresa, and the final realization that this love is
impossible. The characters are comparable to those of Racine:
Teresa is Phèdre; Hipólito, Hyppolitus; Alicia, the Anicia added
by Racine to the original cast. In the case of Hipólito and
Alicia, these are obvious Spanish equivalents of the original
names. Teresa is not so close to Phedre, but symbolically, the
ivy of the title refers to her, and the similarity of pronunciation
between *Hiedra* and Fedra, the Spanish form of Phèdre, is
obvious. However, Villaurrutia, while perfectly willing to play
such tricks with words, was incapable of doing so without a
reason, as we have seen in the study of his poetry. The *Hiedra*
is climbing ivy, which finds both its support in others; it is also
a symbol of eternal fidelity. Thus, Villaurrutia has conveyed the
theme of the play, the character of the protagonist, and an
ironic commentary on her nature.

The Ivy is no more merely a modern version of Racine's
classic than was *Invitation to Death* a modern-dress *Hamlet.* The
author has added, cut and changed wherever necessary in his
interpretation of the myth. It is still Phèdre and Hippolytus,
but altered in such a way that it has new expression for contemporary man. The unreturned love of Phedre and her subsequent suicide have been developed into a study of the twisted
threads which make up the lives of human beings. Teresa is a
complex psychological entity, torn between her devotion to
Hipólito and growing awareness that she is slowly draining him

of all semblance of individuality. Even more, she finally realizes the nature of the sublimated quasi-incestuous drive which is leading them to a break with the past, and realizes, too, that memories and guilt cannot be left behind when the suitcases are packed, like a pair of old shoes. Phèdre's suicide becomes an even more appalling and yet somehow magnificent spiritual suicide by a woman who is at once malignant and good.

The critic José Luis Martínez has seen here a deliberately anti-heroic resolution, an attempt to express the impossibility of tragedy in the modern world. Certainly, *The Ivy* has nothing of the splendor of *Phèdre* or the vengeance of an angry fate, and it is possible that Villaurrutia may have had something like this in mind. Martínez is correct in his recognition of the impossibility of following Racine even to "the ghost of a Hyppolitus dead by the rage required of the gods . . ."[24] and to Teresa's " 'fury' which she must drown in suicide . . .,"[25] but it seems hardly likely that Villaurrutia's primary intention was any such demonstration. The very nature of the characters makes any other ending impossible; further, do not the very names of our psychological concepts indicate a profound link between our recognition of their role in our destinies and, simultaneously, what the ancients often really meant when they spoke of the gods' interference in the lives of mortals?[26]

The basic image of the play is that of Teresa as the ivy, which feeds parasitically on other life forms. This image is emphasized by the author's directions at the time of her first entrance:

Teresa is about thirty-five. She is tall and strong. One might say that beneath her vegetal-colored skin circulates sap instead of blood. The air and light confuse her and make her feel more intensely. One might also say that from all the objects she touches, all the beings she embraces, she extracts, insensibly, something which enriches her. And we can guess that complete darkness and solitude would impoverish her definitively.[27]

Villaurrutia makes frequent use of this imagery in the dialogue. Perhaps the best and most representative example is the following passionate description by Ernesto, who has loved her quietly and hopelessly. At the same time that it expresses this basic note of Teresa's personality, it reveals Ernesto's longing.

Teresa is like the ivy: she lives from what she touches, what she embraces. Your father said it with other words: "I feel that I give life, heat and fire to this child." I know beings like Teresa, and I confess that not only is there an immense pleasure in allowing them to lean on us, but also in the faintness that follows that transfusion of blood, of sap, in which their contact with us is transformed. It is enough to feel one of their hands rest on yours or seize it, to feel that mysterious transfusion establish itself.[28]

Alone in the house in which she drew on the vitality of her husband, Teresa is physically and spiritually ill; she insists on drawing the curtains and wears a shawl. Eagerly, she anticipates Hipólito's return, perhaps unknowingly half in love already, perhaps, like the ivy, sending out tendrils for support and sustenance. Hipólito himself has been studying abroad for ten years, since, as a reserved child of twelve, he bitterly resented his father's remarriage, and Teresa is both anxious and afraid. But Hipólito proves friendly, warm and tractable; his return provides the vital source on which to draw, and Teresa lays aside her mourning. This change is entirely to the good, for there is a corresponding alteration in Hipólito. His laugh becomes more reserved; the vitality which he exuded begins to desert him, and his promises to Alicia go unobserved. Finally, he capitulates to the as yet imperfectly realized love which has enslaved them. He is too weak to confess to Teresa his engagement to Alicia, too weak to answer Alicia's complaints directly.

The three major figures of this triangle, Alicia, Teresa, and Hipólito, show no clearly defined lines of right or wrong. Julia, Alicia's mother, is malevolent, gossiping, and vicious, while the faithful Ernesto, who serves as an ironic counterpoint to Teresa and whose comments at times echo the classical chorus, is sufficiently strong to put aside his own love for Teresa and counsel her to leave with Hipólito. But Alicia, Teresa, and Hipólito are both right and wrong; they are strong and weak, selfish and generous. Teresa has very nearly destroyed them all, but her final act of renunciation, although it dooms her, gives her the knowledge that she has freed Hipólito. Alicia, caught in the trap forged by Julia to be the undoing of Teresa, is pregnant, and Hipólito has abandoned her. But Alicia has her unborn child to sustain her, and through the struggle with

Teresa, she has freed herself of her mother's domination. She alone walks free and purged from the inferno which has wracked the group. Only Hipólito has no consolation for the empty future. Hippolytus' death here becomes a spiritual destruction, but he has the alternative of rebirth by forcing himself to live again. At least, his death can depend only on him; no god will forge monsters to slay him. He has only to conquer the monsters which surge from his own memory, and he will be free.

It is obvious that whatever may have been Villaurrutia's intent, *The Ivy* is very close to the tragic spirit in its portrayal of spirits wracked by their own torments. At the same time, this entire struggle, the whole tragic encounter, springs from the delicate balance on which good and evil are measured out in our daily lives.

Our lives are always in unstable equilibrium. Good and evil are the weights of the balance. One day we decide—or someone decides for us—not to go on doing the evil which we have done someone. But the evil does not disappear. The evil goes on being the same, except that now it is exercised in a different direction, it falls on another person who in the majority of cases is innocent.[29]

And the fatality of being human is summed up:

To wish to do good and only good, would be the same as going out to the street on a sunny day and trying to keep our bodies from casting a shadow.[30]

The structure of *The Ivy* is carefully developed within a realistic framework; there is no hint of the elements of fantasy which mark *Invitation to Death*. Aside from the unhappy cliché of using the two housemaids to set the scene, it is realistic and professional without falling into routine. One of the effective devices, which we have seen previously in *Invitation to Death*, is the use of parallelistic tableaux. Act I closes with Teresa sitting quietly, murmuring in a barely audible voice, "I am alone! I am alone again!"[31] Act II closes with a similar scene, except that now, when we have seen Hipólito slowly distintegrate and Teresa's rejuvenation, it is Hipólito who sits quietly, as Teresa caresses him.

Another telling device is the use of concrete objects which serve as points of dramatic reference. Just as the coffin of *Invitation to Death* looms behind the action of the play, so we see Teresa first in a shawl which emphasizes her spiritual state. At the end of the play, in a telling repetition of an action which has characterized her throughout the first act, she sits caressing the velvet of the sofa, and the play ends as she sits once more enveloped in her shawl; she watches Hipólito leave and weeps, surrounded by the musty relics of her doubly thwarted love.

The following year, 1942, *The Legitimate Wife (La mujer legítima)* won second prize in a drama competition sponsored by the Ideal Theater. A number of critics censured Villaurrutia sharply for what they considered a compromise; José Luis Martínez accused him of succumbing to the temptations of the commercial theater.[32] The justice of this attack is somewhat dubious; in order for the experimental theater to have been of any real value, given the condition of the Mexican stage, it had to become a force within the commercial theater, and this could hardly take place without adjusting to the patterns of this theater. A compromise it certainly was, but not the sellout which critics attacked. As *Invitation to Death* and the earlier efforts of Ulises and Orientación had clearly demonstrated, the Mexican public was simply not ready for anything resembling overt dramatic innovation.

In any event, while neither *The Legitimate Wife* nor later plays reveal any corruption of taste or skill, Villaurrutia does use standard practices, clichés of the boulevard theater, such as the two maids of *The Ivy. The Legitimate Wife* is by no means the masterpiece which Enrique Diez-Canedo would have us believe it to be in his prologue to the 1943 edition. It lies well above the routine of Mexican theatrical fare in the 1940's, but well below Villaurrutia's capabilities.

The work deals with the rivalry between Sara, long the mistress of Rafael, who has now married her after the death of his first wife, and Marta, Rafael's resentful and volcanic daughter, who is violently opposed to what she rightly regards as the legitimizing of an adulterous liaison and the installation of Sara in her home, thereby sullying her mother's memory. Although Marta apparently becomes reconciled to this situation, she is constantly plotting against Sara, and when her effort to make

Sara appear as having betrayed Rafael fails, we find that Marta suffers from the same congenital mental illness which had made Rafael's marriage a torment and had driven him to Sara for solace. Ironically, although Marta's plot fails, Rafael's weakness of character is revealed in his initial suspicion of Sara, and the latter insists on leaving him, aware of the impossibility of finding happiness in this tormented household. Fortunately, Villaurrutia's bid for commercial success did not lead him into the pitfall of the happy ending, nor does Sara flounce out in an uncharacteristic high moral tone. He realized that the personalities of Rafael and Sara would be out of harmony with any facile resolution, and ended the play on an open note.

There are strong similarities between *The Legitimate Wife* and *The Ivy*. In each, the focal personage is a stepmother. In the earlier play, the problem was the quasi-incestuous love of stepmother for stepson, which boiled just below the surface, while in *The Legitimate Wife*, it is the hatred directed toward the second wife by her stepdaughter. There is also the same interest in abnormal types; Marta is even more abnormal than any of the characters of *The Ivy*. Unfortunately, she has neither the compelling attraction nor the plausibility of Teresa; she is so malevolent that her few moments of seeming friendliness are immediately suspect.

The strongest character is Sara. A trifle shopworn, she is both fiercely self-protective and profoundly understanding. Rafael is understanding but weak, dramatically insufficient, while the other characters are of little importance except for Marta's brother Angel, who becomes important only in the closing act. The value of the play lies not in the characters, but in experimentation with technique, in spite of certain clichés. The language is more restrained, less "poetic," as Villaurrutia sought the proper expression for his drama. Fortunately, he realized that "natural" language was not his own dramatic language, and in later plays returned to the mode of expression of *The Ivy*, a modified form of the language of the more experimental works.

The experimentation in technique and structure follows certain lines laid down earlier and visible in much of Villaurrutia's theater. There is, for example, the quite remarkable use of a portrait of the dead wife to symbolize Marta's relentless struggle. She removes the picture before Sara's arrival and even during the months of feigned friendship refuses to replace it. Sara, in turn, focuses on this portrait as a symbol of her determination to remain. The final speech of Act I crystallizes these two attitudes, demonstrating the importance of this use of concrete object as dramatic metaphor.

It was a very human and very beautiful impulse to take away that portrait! But now, Marta, that you know what I think, you can put it again where it has always been . . . where it will always be![33]

After Marta has succeeded in causing a breach between Sara and Rafael, she returns the portrait to its place, and Sara understands.

So that, from the portrait, she can see me leave . . . just as, the day I came to this house [Marta] took it down, so she could not see me enter. . . .[34]

Structurally, *The Legitimate Wife* follows the usual realistic pattern of presentation, complication and resolution, without any of the slowly unfolding tragic sense of *The Ivy*. No one is cleansed or purged, and the characters are damned to go on living in their individual infernos. There is a jarring device in the use of an anonymous letter accusing Sara of an adulterous affair. This letter is, of course, false, concocted by Marta's literally insane jealousy. Díez-Canedo, in his overly defensive prologue, feels that Marta's insanity justifies the use of the letter—this is not quite the same thing as the accusing letter which is the stock resource of back writers. He is quite right, but this fact does not save the letter from being unnecessarily conventional, nor does it justify Rafael's surprising willingness to take it at face value, especially in view of the fact that he alone, of all the characters, knows of the mental instability of Marta.

In *The Legitimate Wife* there is again a good sense of the theatrical, the proper ending to a dramatic act. Both acts end on scenes of exultation: Sara's proclamation of her intent to take her rightful place (hence the ironic title); her emotional collapse after the discovery of her supposed affair; and the final moments in which a suddenly humanized Angel hovers protectively over a bewildered Marta. Again, these scenes are in the nature of tableaux. The first act curtain falls after Sara has finished speaking and stands looking at Marta "with a look in which there is not the least shadow of pity or of triumph but an intense and profound understanding."[35] In Act II, she weeps alone, after the united and disapproving family have left, arm in arm. The final act ends on the ironic tableau in which Angel and Marta re-create a scene which the house has known many times. In each case there is a suspension of action, a moment which is static but permeated with dramatic tension.

In *El yerro candente (The Burning Error)*,[36] written and staged in 1944, Villaurrutia turns again to orthodox realistic drama. The play revolves primarily about the relationships between Antonia, her father Eduardo and her uncle Román, and, as the plot develops, the increasingly curious relationships between Eduardo, Román, and Antonia's mother explode. Eventually Antonia faces the knowledge that her biological father is Román and that Eduardo married her pregnant mother out of love and compassion. The theme is the question of rightful paternity: whether the true parent, who has abandoned her, or the adoptive parent has the real right. This is not a legal or technical quibble; Antonia must choose between the man who has been her father and the uncle who suddenly usurps his place.[37]

The Burning Error, however, is not simply a puzzle. Antonia's choice is never in doubt. The emphasis lies rather on the clash of personality, as in all Villaurrutia's serious plays. The plot may change, but the essential relationships remain the same, much more so than appears on the surface. In *The Burning Error* we find again the identification of child with parent and the struggle between foster parent and foster child, so much so that the major characters in the plays are equivalent:

The Ivy	*The Legitimate Wife*	*The Burning Error*
Teresa	Sara	Román
The father	The mother	Eduardo
Hipólito	Marta	Antonia

In each of these cases, one of the characters is attempting to win the affections of a foster child. The variations are considerable from one work to another; the relationships sometimes imply love, sometimes only antagonism. However, the fundamental relationship remains the same, in spite of skillful variations on the external situation. Román, for instance, is Antonia's true father, while her foster father is Eduardo; this is merely a disguise of the true relationship, since their roles reverse this situation. Other characters are also duplicated: Ernesto of *The Ivy* is much like Rafael of *The Legitimate Wife*, while Eduardo is strongly reminiscent of both, although his role in this scheme is somewhat different. Antonia is a re-creation of both Eduardo and Román, with each of whom she has characteristics in common: the dignity and intelligence of the former, the hidden strength of the latter. This patterning of the children after the parents also exists in *The Ivy*, between Hipólito and his dead father, as the other characters point out, and to a lesser degree, between Alicia and Julia. In *The Legimate Wife*, Marta is very closely identified with her mother, Angel with his father. Frequently, this identification extends far beyond the simple presumed inheritance of traits; Marta and Angel, for example, are destined to repeat interminably the pathetic relationship of keeper and patient which was the true nature of their parents' roles.

We have not mentioned *Invitation to Death* in this regard, since its very ancestry presumes these same relationships. Strangely, it is in this play that the focus shifts significantly and the foster parent is reduced to a thoroughly minor role. The magnificent Claudius of *Hamlet* becomes a stuffy, repugnant and altogether second-rate indivdual. He is also the only foster parent—and this is his function, although the liaison is devoid of legal sanction—who is entirely unsympathetic, due to his character, rather than to the insignificance of his role. Sara is one of the most sympathetic and entirely human people in Villaurrutia's theater, Teresa, if not entirely admirable, is understandable; Román, who is a singularly cynical and unpleasant person, achieves a certain pathetic dignity in his last desperate effort to regain his lost soul.

The most interesting aspect of *The Burning Error* is the struggle between Román and Antonia. The latter is typical of Villaurrutia's heroines; she is the most powerful personality in the play, almost masculine in her independent self-assurance. Román's transformation contributes strongly to the play's most powerful scenes, those between him and Antonia. According to a critic who signed himself M. A., this transformation is not properly prepared in the preceding action.[38] However, a careful reading displays how Villaurrutia etched the extreme nervous strain under which Román was acting, and there does not seem to be any inconsistency in his actions.

No small part of the dramatic power of these scenes and of the remaining climactic moments of the play is due to the dialogue, which is among Villaurrutia's best. Stripped of non-essentials, classical in its economy, it achieves a remarkable level of impact. Technically, the play is within the direct realistic pattern which we have come to expect, a realism which focuses on the psychological factors of its struggling characters. Through a gradual revelation of the facts underlying an apparently placid home life, an extraordinary tension is built up, and the actual secret is not revealed until almost the end of the second act. Again, each act ends in a tableau which reflects the emotional involvements of the characters. There is a minimum of stage business; certainly nothing like the telephone call of *Invitation to Death*, the letter or the portrait of *The Legitimate Wife*, or Teresa's shawl in *The Ivy*. There is, however, an excellent verbal equivalent in the scene in which Antonia and Eduardo regret that they cannot take their books with them when they leave. This simple technique reveals the complete alteration to which they must submit; the affectionate joy with which they choose the few they may take is proof that the change will not destroy them.

Villaurrutia's next three-act play, *El pobre Barba Azul* (Poor Bluebeard), written in 1946 and staged the following year, is a complete change from the previous works. Gone are the personality studies and the odd family relationships. This is sheer comedy-farce, divorced from the abrasive tensions of the other plays, and employing almost constantly the tone of sardonic knife-edged humor which exists in even his most serious works. Villaurrutia himself, alluding to the rather overwhelmingly serious nature of the theater of his day, called the play "a smile on the frowning face of the Mexican theater."[39] The chief merit of *Poor Bluebeard* is the tongue-in-cheek gaiety of its absurdly improbable situation. Samuel, recently divorced, becomes engaged to Carmen because the latter wishes to spite

her suitor Alonso. To the dismay of everyone, and most especially
Samuel, the fact that the previously unassailable Carmen wants
him makes him thoroughly desirable to all women, including
his ex-wife, until the confusions are resolved and the amazed
Casanova returns to his previous unloved state. The humor,
compounded of equal parts of situation comedy and repartee,
is close to the Spanish Golden Age in its utter disregard for
probability, its rapid action and sprightly dialogue, although
the model is certainly the French boulevard theater. If serious
matters occasionally appear in *Poor Bluebeard,* they are promptly
converted into comedy.

Each of the characters is a type, and much of the laughter
is due to their typical reactions. Amparo, whose name means
"shelter," is a completely frank and more than a trifle naive
young lady—or at least so she would have it seem—who is more
in need of shelter than able to provide it. Virginia, the gay
divorcee bent on remaining in that lamentable state as briefly
as possible, is thoroughly unvirginal. Beatriz, the very, very
serious young wife of a psychiatrist, interprets everything in
terms of befuddled psychiatric jargon; she is far indeed from
the Beatrice who surely was her source. Luisillo is the amateur
scandalmonger whose great pride is his unprecedented ability
to spread an edifying bit of gossip in an astoundingly brief
time; he is, in a sense, the chorus which clucks about in the
background, commenting on the absurdity of his fellow human
beings and himself. Each of these is a type, and each reacts in a
typical way at all times; yet, the author has managed to breathe
such vivacity into their words that they never cease to be
absurdly, ridiculously, typically human.

The author and the audience enjoy themselves at the expense
of psychoanalysis through the maunderings of Beatriz.

Beatriz: It seems that, at least among a certain social class, in Guadal-
    ajara the psychopathology of daily life is of an incredible variety
    and richness.
Carmen: Beatriz means that in Guadalajara there is a great deal of
    adultery, divorce, elopement and triangles.[40]

Beatriz *(to Don Lucas):* This engagement is so unsuspected. Don't
    you think so? I suspect there's a submerged complex here.[41]

In only two of the characters, Carmen and Samuel, is there any individuality. Carmen is notable throughout most of the play chiefly because she is more sharp-witted than the others, a veritable model of the sophisticated young woman. In answer to a thrust by Virginia, and aided by Amparo's usual bluntness, she deftly turns the verbal dagger into a boomerang.

Beatriz: Carmen thinks that being single is a quality.
Virginia: Which ceases to be so as time passes. Carmen has cultivated this quality, until now, with great success; but, it seems, she's getting tired, aren't you, dear?
Carmen (*firmly*): If I'm getting tired of it or not, is my concern and only mine. I have never pointed out that after getting tired of being single, you got tired of being married and, now that you are divorced, you are beginning to show signs of fatigue again.
Amparo: The Marathon of fatigue! Sit down, Virginia. You must be very tired.[42]

Carmen is an inveterate tease. Teasingly, she convinces Samuel that she loves him; once committed to marry him, she teases the poor love-sick Alonso to the point of desperation. Samuel is as hopeless a ninny in affairs of the heart as can be imagined; his sudden transformation into a veritable Don Juan leaves him bewildered but delighted, terrified at the thought that matrimony might again destroy his amorous prowess. He much prefers this wonderful situation, surrounded, even besieged by women. Even Virginia, thoroughly disenchanted with him after their divorce, falls victim to his mythical charm to the extent of engaging in a seductive striptease via telephone. Samuel becomes a symbol of love, but a symbol in joke.

It is only during the final scenes that Carmen and Samuel achieve human stature. Her repentance is surprisingly tender, and his refusal to hold her to her word is remarkably effective. At the moment when she was to have married Samuel, Carmen marries Alonso, and poor Blue Beard is left to say pathetically but with a certain nobility, "It is not necessary to say anything. I know what you are going to say! . . . Go, go away all of you, too. I'll go later. Now, leave this poor, poor Blue Beard alone for a moment."[43]

Samuel is, of course, an ironic parody of the legends of Blue Beard, Don Juan Tenorio and the other great lovers; he is a success in love only because the women wish him to be so and believe that he is so. Without this tacit agreement on the part of his admirers, the lover is stripped of his attractions. Taken in conjunction with the women in his other plays, from María Luisa to the strong figures of Sara or Antonia, there is also more than a hint that Villaurrutia's attitude toward the relationships between the sexes is strongly Shavian. Without imputing to Villaurrutia any attitudes quite so overt as those demonstrated by Shaw in *Man and Superman*, the Mexican dramatist's strongest characters are, in general, female; even Teresa, who cannot exist without drawing sustenance from those about her, becomes in her relationship with Hipólito, as she was with his dead father, the dominant figure. In *The Burning Error* and *The Legitimate Wife*, Antonia and Sara are the key figures; the denouement depends on them, it is they who control the situations.

Villaurrutia's last full-length play was *Juego peligroso* (Dangerous Game), first performed in 1950. It is a curious brittle piece about the supposed infidelity of Arturo, whose wife Irene, upon returning from a trip, finds a piece of strange jewelry among her own possessions. Accepting this as conclusive evidence of Arturo's betrayal, she sets in motion an ornate machinery in which she confesses to Arturo that she loves another, thereby hoping to force him to sue for divorce. At the same time, she attempts to discover the owner of the jewelry, and it is finally identified as belonging to her close friend, Celia. Finally, the whole plot is revealed to be a conspiracy by Celia's husband Francisco, who had hoped to use the jewelry as proof of his own wife's infidelity and Arturo's treachery, thus freeing both himself and Irene, whom he loves.

The artificiality of the plot is obvious; neither Arturo nor especially Irene behave in a reasonable manner. To what extent we might have expected them to do so, given the atmosphere of sophisticated skirting of adultery which seems to be the chief concern of all the characters, is doubtful. Certainly, this is one of the author's weakest works in terms of human motivation and reaction. Equally surely, the work is a criticism of this artificial brittleness. The dangerous game of the title refers to Irene's perilous (and foolish) machinations and to Francisco's plotting; it refers equally to the superficial game of playing with infidelity which all the characters engage in. The first scene sets the tone, as all the husbands joke about their presumed seductive powers, and there is a strong hint that much of this banter is extremely pointed.

As stated, *Dangerous Game* is one of Villaurrutia's weakest plays; further, although it has clear antecedents as far back as *The Moment Has Arrived,* it is atypical in its melodramatic exposition and resolution. Although the same general attitude prevails in *Poor Blue Beard,* the comic tone makes amusing what in *Dangerous Game* borders on mass neurosis. The key human relationships of most of the serious works are lacking. Although Irene too is involved in a search for truth, as are almost all of Villaurrutia's protagonists, the search here is melodramatic, an external problem to be solved, rather than a basic search for the significance underlying human existence. As such, *Dangerous Game* must be regarded as at best a qualified and partial success.

During this period of concentration on the full-length play, Villaurrutia continued to be interested in the possibilities of the play in one act. In 1945, he adapted Schnitzler's short story *Der Tod des Junggesellen,* staged in 1946 as *El solterón* (The Bachelor). The source is particularly interesting, since extensive changes were necessary in order to adapt it for the stage. It is, in fact, a combination of translation, adaptation and original invention. The plot is the well-known story of the bachelor who has left a deathbed confession of his illicit relationship with the wife of one of his friends, without specifying which wife or which friend; Villaurrutia took this plot complete from Schnitzler, making virtually no changes except for the ending. It is, however, this ending which stamps the play with originality. Instead of the note of tawdry pessimism and betrayal which Schnitzler chose, Villaurrutia invented a second letter in which the dead friend confessed that his original confession had been one final practical joke. Thus, the triple domestic tragedy is transformed into a Pirandellian enigma. Like the characters of *Cosí è (se vi pare),* the dead man's friends can never really resolve their dilemma; each must choose a reality which he can accept.

The conversion from short story to theater involved more radical changes. In the original, each character reacts to the realization of the betrayal by indulging in an interior monologue on the erotic relationship between husband and wife, a

typical theme in Schnitzler's work. On the stage, however, the
characters have no such recourse without resorting to the aside,
a trick with which Villaurrutia would have no dealings. In order
to avoid this pitfall, he eliminated the husband-wife relationship
entirely and had the characters suggest their emotional reactions through dialogue and physical action. During the reading
of the first letter, Villaurrutia indicates the individual reactions
through stage directions, and the reactions of the Doctor (extreme nervousness), the Businessman (anxiety) and the Poet
(an ironic humor which is replaced by considerable reluctance
as the full import of the letter strikes him).

In his adaptation, Villaurrutia faced the problem of creating
the necessary mood. Without the resources of description or
the internal monologue, he again had to rely on visual and
aural effects. The stage setting contributes considerably to this
mood. Instead of the actual presence of the dead man, Villaurrutia used the door to his bedroom, placed in the most
commanding position, center stage rear. In this position, it
becomes a symbol of the dead man dominating the stage just as
he dominates the action. It is the center of reference; the
characters cast uneasy glances at it and what lies behind it,
and as they become enraged over their betrayal by their dead
friend, they direct their protests toward the door. Although the
character of the servant Juan is also important in that his silent
movements and muffled voice aid considerably in sustaining
the mood, one of the most effective devices is the trick of
having the Doctor's voice audible during Juan's phone call,
notifying him of the death. It was necessary to create the situation of the Bachelor's death and to make clear to the audience
the odd circumstances; at the same time, Schnitzler's method
was out of the question, since the shift of scene necessary for
the servant's visit to the doctor would be disastrous to the
unity of the play. The call also fulfills another important function. Any diversion of audience interest during the early moments, when the play is weakest, would be fatal. The telephone
call, almost certainly inspired by Cocteau's *La voix humaine,*
which makes brilliant use of the instrument although in a
different way, creates immediate tension and attracts interest
until the situation itself is sufficiently developed.

The process of adaptation required omission, as well as addition and alteration, but the most significant change is in the divergence from Schnitzler's ending. In Schnitzler, the Poet decides on suicide as the only answer to his problem. Even here, he is possessed by his own sense of the melodramatic. He makes certain that the damning letter is in his pocket, imagining his wife's pride in his nobility when she finds it safely sealed among his papers. Villaurrutia's addition of the second letter alters the situation considerably and makes this resolution dramatically impossible. Instead, he had the Poet search frantically for the letter and constructed the silent but highly effective ending in which the three leave gesturing their complicity in the conspiracy of silence.

> The Poet: Good night, doctor. (*And then with an almost imperceptible shudder, in a tone which cannot avoid being of painful complicity, he adds*): As far as this matter is concerned, I won't say anything to my wife *either*.[44]

The characters of *The Bachelor* are almost completely typed, and these semicaricatures provide the only relief from the drama of the situation in the satire of their typicity. Thus, the Businessman forgets the presumed infidelity of his wife in his eagerness to learn the nature of his inheritance; the Poet's every movement is satire, from the grandiloquence of his emotion over his friend's death to the conspiratorial attitude of his last speech. Only the Doctor escapes this typing; he is disturbed by the peculiar incidents prior to the discovery of the letter, and his reaction to its disclosures is a completely human blend of horror, disbelief, anger, and revulsion.

Despite the years which had intervened, *The Bachelor* is in the vein of *Incredible* and *What Are You Thinking About?* It is, like these earlier works, an enigma, a mystery. Which of the two letters is the joke, and what future course each may have to take in the light of this Pirandellian dilemma, is for each of the characters to decide for himself, just as the befuddled husband of *Incredible* must make his own decision, must *act* in the face of the cataclysmic revelation which has put an end to the placidity of his previous domestic life. Which reality to accept, the easy acceptance of the second letter, with its consequent continued status quo, or the difficult acceptance of the first letter as authentic, with the necessary corollary of doubt and anguish; the easy oblivion of the mushroom or the tragic search of the human being: all this existential anguish lies beneath the apparently facile surface of *The Bachelor,* just as it lies beneath much of Villaurrutia's work.

La tragedia de las equivocaciones (The Tragedy of Errors) was written and produced in 1950; its title is, obviously, a pun on Shakespeare's *Comedy of Errors.* It is a one-act monodrama, presenting Villaurrutia's restless imagination with an entirely new set of problems. Orthodox techniques of lighting, staging, and the like, are feasible, but in the monodrama the question of physical action becomes more important than ever. A static stage makes it difficult for the single actor to retain the attention of the audience; at the same time, constant movement places too heavy a demand on the actor. There is also the prosaic but essential problem of conveying the necessary antecedents; since only one character speaks or, usually, is seen, ordinary techniques cannot be employed. The commonest means of overcoming these difficulties is through the use of some external apparatus, such as a radio or a telephone. The latter is used brilliantly in one of the models of the genre, Cocteau's *La voix humaine,* while the radio provides the sounding board for the single character in the Mexican Díez Barroso's *E o F,* and the Cuban Nora Badía uses a mute character in another extremely effective monodrama, *Tomorrow Is a Word.*[45] Villaurrutia chose to attack the problem at its original source, the monologue. In *The Tragedy of Errors,* the stage is bare, the curtain down. The actor enters from behind the curtain and proceeds to speak directly to the audience. Even in this formalized approach, Villaurrutia recognized the need for physical movement. The actor leaves the stage momentarily in his role as Cosme, reappears temporarily in the role of Damián, Cosme's twin, then reappears as Cosme to finish his story. The success of this approach to the monodrama is questionable. Although perhaps serviceable in itself, it does not represent a direction in which this minor subgenre may develop, in comparison with the daring innovations of such dramatists as Evreinov, particularly in his *Vkulisak Dushi (The Theater of the Soul).*

Like many of Villaurrutia's plays, *The Tragedy of Errors* is not resolved. Cosme's future course of action in the face of his brother's assumption of his identity at key moments is still a mystery as he shrugs his shoulders wonderingly and exits. Although the source of the play is unquestionably Shakespeare, and through him, the whole tradition of the confusion between identical twins which was used so extensively in the Latin comedy, various philosophical themes are suggestively inter-mingled. Their absolute opposition in every regard except their total physical identity suggests the Platonic theory of the two halves into which the whole is separated when it is born into this world. There is also a hint of the *doppelganger,* the familiar spirit who is one with us and must be preserved at all costs even though he is frequently malevolent. Unfortunately, within the frame of the monolgue, these themes are hardly more than suggested, and the *Tragedy of Errors* remains an amusing ex-periment without likely descendants or real significance.

In addition to writing for the stage, Villaurrutia also pre-pared a series of film scenarios and won two awards; unfor-tunately, these scripts seem to have been lost, along with an early musical comedy which he wrote. One script, *La mulata de Córdoba* (The Mulata of Cordoba), is included in the sec-ond edition of the complete works, along with an opera libretto based on the same myth, written in collaboration with Agustín Lazo. The basic story is that of a woman in league with the Devil, who destroys the families which have rejected her by enslaving the men, father and son, and forcing the latter to abandon his bride. Since the script was written in 1944, while Villaurrutia was actively engaged in writing for the professional stage, it provides an interesting point of comparison. In addition, he also published an article on the differences between living theater and the film,[46] in which he examines the usual positions in regard to this difference and finds that they represent a difference of degree rather than of kind. It must be remembered that Villaurrutia wrote well before the development of the nonrealistic film, as exemplified in the work of Bergman, Fellini, and others, and that had he lived, he might well have seen fit to change his opinion somewhat. Villaurrutia points out that the assertion that the distinction lies in the motion pictures' possibilities for rejecting unities of time and space is inaccurate,

102 XAVIER VILLAURRUTIA

since the theater of Lope de Vega and Shakespeare ignored
them even more completely. Nor, he feels, is the difference to
be found in the stage's emphasis on the spoken word and the
film's reliance on visual material; he points out that wordiness,
even the brilliant wordiness of a Shaw, is as harmful to the play
as the film's reliance on silent interlude can be to the picture.

The true difference lies, feels Villaurrutia, in the one element
which is integral to the film and does not exist in the live
theater—the camera. This mechanical addition makes it possible
for the motion picture audience to see the action from physical
angles which are forbidden the audience of a play. Closeups,
pan shots, dissolves, and so on, all contribute to the total effect
of the film, and they are effects impossible in the live theater.
In addition to the changes of perspective which are made
possible in this fashion, there is also the purely technical matter
of the opportunity to carefully select the elements which are
to make up the final film. This process of retakes, cutting, and
editing allows what Villaurrutia called "a surprising concentration of space and time."[47]

We would expect, then, to find that the *Mulata of Córdoba*
differs from the commercial plays only in regard to camera
possibilities, since cutting and editing are not the function of
the scenarist. We must also remember that such matters as
closeups and camera angles are generally the province of the
director, so that in essence the motion picture script is a theatrical
script, with the addition of such camera directions as the author
may deem necessary. This is exactly what we find in the *Mulata*;
it differs from the plays of the same period only in the panoramic
scale on which much of the action takes place, and in the
dramatic use of photographic angles. Among the techniques
used to best effect is the traveling camera; as we are introduced
to each household, the camera recedes, turns to the window
and passes through it. This is followed by a dissolve and a
transition to the next household. More dramatic, in the strict
sense of the word, are the use of the camera to sweep the interior
of the church during the wedding and the use of landscape shots
for the setting of mood. Two incidents which are dramatically
necessary to the film also rely on the camera: at one point it
swoops to the hiding place of Jorge Reyes, thus pointing out
that Sara will soon learn of latest developments through her

secret ally's eavesdropping. The other is the device of having the camera follow closely behind Sara's unknown lover, creating, through a distortion of perspective, an illusion of enormous physical size.

None of these techniques can be considered radical, particularly in view of technical developments in the film and the use of the camera in the last fifteen years, and the *Mulata of Córdoba* can be considered almost as though it were written for the stage, although its subject matter is radically different from anything Villaurrutia wrote for the stage. The fact that the work is based on a folk tale whose mood had to be maintained, even though the plot was altered drastically, may account for the lack of motivation for Sara's final departure. Her malignant influence on the provincial village of Rincón Brujo has, after all, been equally the fault of others, and she seems genuinely in love. We can only lament the fact that the author did not have a freer hand to develop the conflict. Curiously, the earlier operatic version of the same legend shows little similarity of treatment. The theme of the opera is much closer to the legend, and the plot is almost unrecognizably different. The aura of satanic mystery and final magical disappearance of the *Mulata* Soledad are noticeably lacking in the film script, which is at times uncomfortably close in spirit to the stock provincial melodrama which was long a staple of Mexican film.

An important thematic characteristic of Villaurrutia's theater has been pointed out by Donald Shaw in his "Passion and Truth in Villaurrutia's Theater."[48] Shaw sees a predominance in Villaurrutia's plays of human passions: love, hatred, jealousy, and so on. (Although his insistence on this aspect is most important, this writer is inclined to disagree with his acceptance of Torres-Ríoseco's assessment of the poetry as lacking in human passion. There are different kinds of involvement, which is, after all, what Shaw is talking about.) Further, he believes these passionate onsets to be closely related to the notion of the discovery of a truth, which he considers to be closely related to sincerity, pointing out that the base characters in Villaurrutia's theater are, above all, those who are insincere. This theme certainly marks many of the plays. The protagonists are, above all, faithful to themselves, authentic human beings who exert every possible effort to function "authentically" in the face of the hypocritical actions of their opposing characters: Sara versus Marta, for example.

If we examine further this effort at sincerity and authenticity in Villaurrutia's plays, we also see that the dramatic action frequently revolves about a secret: the insanity of Marta's mother in *The Legitimate Wife*, the real nature of Teresa's attraction to Hipólito in *The Ivy*, the secret of Antonia's birth in *The Burning Error*, the secret in *Dangerous Game*. The best developed example of the secret is in *Invitation to Death*, where the primary secret, the fate of Alberto's father, is never overtly resolved, but the real dramatic action revolves about an entirely different secret, that of Alberto's inevitable fascination, his unavoidable commitment to death. It is discovery of this secret which provides the true subject of the play; more, it is the gradual revelation of the threads which make up the pattern of Alberto's life which create an air strikingly similar to the hints provided by Tiresias in *Oedipus Rex* prior to the final cataclysm of Oedipus' knowledge of his sin. Certainly, Alberto is no Oedipus, any more than he is Hamlet; he does, however, share with the archetypal figure of Greek tragedy the same determination to find his truth, in the face of grievous warnings, just as he shares with the greatest figure of English tragedy the mocking recognition of his too human failings. Villaurrutia's plays, with the possible exception of *Invitation to Death*, are certainly not tragedies in the usual sense of the word; many are very close to domestic dramas, to what Alfredo Cardona Peña has called "the study of certain moral or immoral aspects of the well-to-do middle class."[49] However, if we accept Francis Fergusson's theory of tragedy as the "tragic rhythm of action,"[50] of the three tragic moments of purpose, passion, or perception, we recognize that Villaurrutia's protagonists, in their single-minded devotion to finding their individual truths, are very close to the tragic spirit, and Alberto's heroic flight in search of himself, his recognition and final renunciation to death are very much in the tragic mold.

CHAPTER 4

Influence and Originality

In studying the work of any creative artist, the critic encounters the thorny problem of the influences which have helped shape the work. To assess a work as though it were the sum of a series of influences is to deny its most important formal aspect: the unity of conception and creation which gives it cohesion. To regard the work as unique, isolating it without regard to other works, is to disregard its position in the continuum of art. The nature and degree of influences vary widely, and in the contemporary period particularly, where there are certain common patterns of interest and a tacit cultural patrimony, coincidence is a further complicating factor. This problem becomes extraordinarily involved when dealing with a figure as cosmopolitan as Villaurrutia, thoroughly conversant with European and Mexican literature and art. Further, he was the product of a period in Mexican letters which was nearly as tumultuous as the political and social upheavals which accompanied it.

Villaurrutia was not excepted from the attacks of critics who confused art with propaganda and who were unable to perceive the essential Mexican qualities of the work of the "Contemporáneos." Even after his editions of the poetry of Sor Juana and López Velarde, and his study of the latter, which was the key step in the re-evaluation of the author of *Suave patria* and is still a basic source for the proper understanding of his work, Villaurrutia was regarded in some quarters as a Frenchified dilettante. Yet, a careful reading of his work reveals clearly that it must be understood as springing from both sources. It belongs both to the European tradition and to the Mexican, and it is unified by his ability to assimilate and transform these sources.

I   *Villaurrutia and the Theater*

Considering that the avowed purpose behind the organization of Teatro Ulises was the revitalizing of a stagnant theater, it is not surprising that the bulk of the repertory of Ulises and its follower and heir, Orientación, should be composed of foreign works. However, once Villaurrutia began to compose original works for the theater, we find that within a relatively short time his work betrays no clear pattern of influences. The earliest of the *Autos profanos* are clearly influenced by Pirandello's vision of the relativity of reality and, perhaps, by Bergsonian notions of relativity of time; yet, the sharpness of expression is far removed from the tone of Pirandello, and the later *Autos* betray none of this heritage. In the three-act plays, Villaurrutia took his themes more or less ready-made, but adapted and revised them until the finished works were original creations, often far removed from the original sources. It is almost pointless to cite Shakespeare as an influence on *Invitation to Death; Hamlet* forms part of every civilized man's patrimony, and the key fact of Villaurrutia's play is the radical fashion in which it departs from the Hamlet theme.

In his search for universality of expression in which to frame his studies of a specific sector of Mexican society, Villaurrutia undoubtedly learned from many dramatists; yet there is little in his later work which can be ascribed to direct influence. There are still traces of Pirandello in the love for the enigma and the interest in multiple aspects of personality; there is the interest in abnormal psychology which might have been learned in Duhamel or Lenormand, both authors whose work Villaurrutia knew, but might also have been learned in multitudes of other sources. There are strong similarities in the tone of the works to the theater of character as developed by Ruiz de Alarcón, but the differences in intent, the obsessive fixation on certain behavior patterns make Villaurrutia's work far different from that of his seventeenth-century fellow Mexican. As Celestino Gorostiza has pointed out, it is virtually impossible to define influences on Villaurrutia's theater.[1] Rather, he learned from the reading of the masters of European drama, distilling and refining within a framework which is markedly Mexican.

II *The Poetry*

The question of influence on Villaurrutia's poetry is distinctly different. Where his theater seems to be rather a distillation in which we find no obvious echoes, his poetry has provoked affirmations that those who were influential at some stage of his development included Rilke, Cocteau, Gide, Valéry, Samain, Jammes, Baudelaire, Mallarmé, Supervielle, Sor Juana Inés de la Cruz, Quevedo, Juan Ramón Jiménez, López Velarde, and Heidegger. Villaurrutia himself has added the name of a painter, Chirico. It is perfectly obvious that any poet whose work was marked by such an agglomeration of echoes would be little of a poet indeed. Many of the above are visible in some of the earlier poems and represent early influences of tone or vocabulary which soon disappeared. Among these, Juan Ramón Jiménez has often been cited, while Villaurrutia himself confessed that his earliest poems were little more than copies of Albert Samain. In *Reflections* he had already outgrown these early influences. There is none of the delicate beauty of Samain here; rather, the book lies in the tradition of brief, almost impressionist lyrics which dominated much of poetry in English, Spanish, and French at the time. There are traces of Jiménez, a certain similarity in the delicate nostalgia of such poems as "Solitude" and "Portrait," but already the individual personality of the young poet was breaking away in search of its own expression. There is nothing of Jiménez in such lines as "How sweet the water dissolving salts!"[2]

There is sometimes a similarity to Jiménez' work in the compression of image and the use of color as a reflection of the poet's emotional state, but here again the germ of the unmistakable imagery of *Nostalgia of Death* is apparent.

> You were like the water
> a face moved, ¡ay!,
> cut
> by the metal of the reflections.[3]
>   ("Reflejos")

These early influences may fairly be ascribed to the atmosphere in which a young Mexican of poetic talent found himself. It would have been virtually impossible for any poet writing in Spanish to escape some passing influence of Jiménez, just as so many young poets would later be influenced by Garcia Lorca. Samain and the other Symbolists would naturally have been included in the young poet's natural reading, and it is obvious that neither of these exercised any appreciable influence on Villaurrutia.

Many of the alleged influences are rather more cultural orientation than specific influence as such. If Gide, Mallarmé, and Valéry influenced Villaurrutia, it was as men devoted to their rigorous art, alert to the nuances of each word, intellectually omnivorous, unwilling to compromise their esthetic integrity. In this sense, the old charge of Villaurrutia's francophilia is true. He saw in French literature a tradition of rigor and craftsmanship which directed his own attempts to achieve a comparable rigor in his own art. In this connection, we must recall his own statement that the most influential Mexican writers on his generation were González Martínez, Tablada, and López Velarde, the first as a model of poetic integrity, the second as a symbol of the poet's need to be alert to all that was new, the last because he discovered a new face of Mexico and a new expression for it. It would be absurd to see any influence of González Martínez' sententious Symbolism or Tablada's eager attention to poetic fashion in Villaurrutia's own work. The case of López Velarde is much the same; although some of Villaurrutia's earliest poems display clear reminiscences of López Velarde's vocabulary, this soon disappeared. If there is any substantive influence of López Velarde on Villaurrutia, it is in the clarity of vision with which each mercilessly dissected his own spiritual world.

Many of the alleged influences on Villaurrutia lie rather in the fact that certain writers are part of our occidental tradition, part of every writer's daily cultural baggage. This is true, for example, of Baudelaire. In his study, "Villaurrutia and Baudelaire,"[4] Robert Nugent finds some occasional similarities, but concludes that "there is little evidence of a direct imitation of Baudelaire by Villaurrutia. As is generally true in France, Baudelaire's influence is indirect, through a similarity of approach to problems of love, death, dream."[5]

An undeniable influence on the formal structure of much of Villaurrutia's poetry is to be found in the rigidly controlled poetry of the Baroque, and almost certainly directly in Sor Juana. This relationship is obvious in the form of the sonnets and *décimas* and in many of his most characteristic techniques: the insistence on the contrastive conceit, on the play on words, widely known Baroque tricks which Villaurrutia used repeatedly even in those poems written in a freer formal structure. César Rodríguez Chicharro has demonstrated that throughout Villaurrutia's poetry, there are examples of his use of parallelism and of correlation, as well as the more commonly recognized techniques.[6] By correlation, we mean that technique in which key words are repeated throughout the poem in the form of synonyms.[7]

Influence on content is extremely difficult to determine. There is an obvious temptation to see the influence of Heidegger in the emphasis on anguish and the fundamental terror which pervades the work; yet, we have Villaurrutia's express statement that although he felt Heidegger to be the philosopher closest to his own preoccupations, he had formulated the body of his thought before reading Heidegger for the first time.[8] A careful reading of the poems is enlightening in this regard. There are certain obvious similarities, such as the interest in the relations between time and existence, the stress on anguish and the effort to comprehend the nature of death, but these are *aspects* of Heidegger's philosophical synthesis, while for Villaurrutia they are the obsessive body of his poetry. Nor need they be more than coincidence; the nature of time is a fundamental theme in contemporary literature, and the themes of anguish and death are not exclusively the property of Heidegger or the various Existentialist schools. It is perhaps reasonable to consider Villaurrutia at least a semi-existentialist, but it would seem that this position was adopted independent of foreign influences.

The tormented nocturnal world of Villaurrutia's poetry has antecedents in other sources. His creation of a world of dreams as partial metaphor, partial equivalent for the nightmare world in which he exists, and the use of sleep as an almost exact duplication of death, are both constants in his work. In sleep the subconscious world of terror surges forth, and the walls between external and internal reality crumble. Life and death, waking and sleeping, are confused. The roots of all this are clearly in the Romantic preoccupation with states of dream and madness, and Villaurrutia himself saw this preoccupation with the dream as at the heart of modern poetry.[9] It is quite possible that his affinities with Supervielle and Cocteau spring as much from their profound interest in this theme as from any influence which might have changed radically Villaurrutia's poetic development. His thesis is that the entire movement has been misunderstood, because of what were really extraneous developments having little to do with the true meaning of the movement. "By virtue of the law of least resistance, everything which is *romantic* has been dangerously reduced to designate, almost always the disorderly, the spontaneous, when it is not verbalism or eloquence."[10]

The true essence of Romanticism is found in the work of such poets as Nerval and Bécquer, who express "restlessness and anguish before the cosmic mystery, nostalgia for the already known, torment before the unknown and the oscillation of the spirit in the worlds of wakefulness and dream."[11] Romanticism in its true manifestation is a "waking of the soul and an awakening to the dream."[12]

These few paragraphs are a clear summing up, or a guide to Villaurrutia's poetry. His work is precisely the opposite of what he objected to in the so-called Romantics; it is cultured, sincere, disciplined. In thematic material it is closely related to the Romanticism of Bécquer, Nerval, and Novalis.

We know from Nandino that Villaurrutia was a dedicated reader of Albert Béguin's *L'âme romantique et le rêve*, first published in 1937, and in his article "Romanticism and the Dream," he states unequivocally his support of Béguin's contention that "every period of human thought could be defined, profoundly, by the relationships which it establishes between dream and waking. . . ."[13] Despite his wholehearted acceptance of the dream state as a major theme, Villaurrutia was a rigidly controlled artist, whose work in this respect lies at the opposite pole from the Surrealists, despite what is often a common subject matter. He specifically rejected automatic writing;[14] José Luis Martínez has perhaps best defined Villaurrutia's difference with the Surrealists when he speaks of "that permanently lucid intelligence, unalterable by passion. . . ."[15] Both Villaurrutia and Supervielle, then, spring from much the same sources and accept and reject the same developments of this

tradition. Curiously, however, although Villaurrutia was a cham-
pion of the dream in Romantic and contemporary poetry and
used it extensively both in his poetry and in *Queen of Hearts,*
he may well have learned its use originally from another source.

. . . There perhaps exists in my work, rather than the influence of
certain writers, that of a painter. In Chirico I found often a clear
affinity.[16]

The close relationship between the bodiless footsteps of a
Villaurrutia nocturne and the menacingly distorted shadows of
Chirico's work is astonishing, particularly in such paintings as
Mystery and Melancholy of a Street which Villaurrutia used as
an illustration in his article on the relationships between live
theater and the fiilm.[17]

III *Villaurrutia and the Poetry of Death*

There are numerous antecedents for Villaurrutia's preoccupation with death in his poetry, but none for the peculiar personal
shading which makes his work distinctive: the personalization
of death to the point where it becomes Death, a uniquely
personal entity. Spanish antecedents sometimes cited are the
mystics and Quevedo, but the latter, the greatest of the Spanish
poets of death, is more interested in the physical fact of the
end of life and the corruption of the body than in Death as the
eternal companion, while for the mystics, death was a means to
an end, a passage to the eternal life, rather than a continuous
presence.

The factor which makes the treatment of death so striking
in Villaurrutia's poetry is the personalization of concept into
being. The only major poet in the Western tradition who has
developed this same concept thoroughly is Rainer Maria Rilke.
Facing an implacable fact of death, they responded in much the
same way.

Who'll show a child just as it is?
Who'll place it within its constellation with the measure of distance in
    its hand?
Who'll make its death from grey bread, that grows hard—or leave it
    there, within the round mouth, like the choking core of a sweet
    apple?

> . . . Minds of murderers are easily divided—but this, though: death,
> the whole of death—even before life's begun, to hold it all so
> gently, and be good: this is beyond description![18]

Certainly there is a strong echo of Villaurrutia in lines such
as these, and in E. M. Butler's comment that "our real destiny,
he maintained, is to die our own death, the death that belongs
to us, that we have carried within us since childhood, and
matured like a fruit."[19] Rilke's words spoken on his deathbed
show his integrity in his faithfulness to this concept: "No: let
me die of my own death. I do not want the death of the
doctors."[20]

There is, however, a corollary to Rilke's attitude toward
death which underlines the considerable difference between
him and the Mexican poet. Rilke's poetry shows clearly that
death, even his personal and private Death, is to be the one
who will open the door to the afterlife which he regards as
the necessary complement, and perhaps even compensation, for
earthly suffering. Even in such a poem as "Requiem," which
superficially appears to be quite close to Villaurrutia's work,
the interest lies in the "afterdeath" rather than in death itself.
There is what might be an anticipation of some of Villaurrutia's
lines in the section entitled "To a Friend," but a close reading
reveals that they are addressed not to Death but to the dead
friend. Both Rilke and Villaurrutia use masks and, notably,
mirrors as symbols of the inability to communicate, but for
Villaurrutia this inability was basic to the condition of existence,
while Rilke transcended it in his semi-mystical states of "pure
being." It is dangerous to pursue too far the use of related
metaphor as a sign of influence. As Elizabeth Sewell comments
in her *Paul Valéry: The Mind in the Mirror* (New Haven, Yale
University Press, 1952, p. 5) "It is a curious and interesting
fact that mirrors become increasingly frequent in literature
toward the end of the nineteenth century." To seek the sources
of Villaurrutia's haunted mirrors in Rilke, or Valéry or Mallarmé
is to lose oneself in a search which has no longer any meaning.
Rilke, a fundamentally anti-Christian but religious poet, went
in search of answers to religious questions; H. F. Peters refers
to his "great trinity of themes: God, love and death."[21] Further,
for Rilke death was a step to "transformation," his theory of

the change of material objects into invisible vibrations, which comes very close to being another kind of immortality, if not precisely the Christian sort. "Death is not the final extinction of personality but the goal and fruition of experience, the crown and seal of living, functional as life itself."²² If for Villaurrutia death was indeed as functional as life, a return to the unknown from which we come, it was certainly no "crown and seal of living"; the fact that phrases such as these could be applied to Rilke illuminates the chasm between the two poets.

Even in poems where Villaurrutia appears to use overtly Rilkean images, "Nocturne of Los Angeles" and "Rose Nocturne," the differences are deep. "Rose Nocturne" is a hymn to the uncreated beauty of the night, of the phantasmagoric world of the dream. In contrast, we find Peters stating that Rilke "found in the rose the symbol in which all these contradictions were jubilantly affirmed because they were seen to arise from a common source, the primordial unity of being. . . ."²³ There is indeed a primordial unity of being in Villaurrutia, but it is the unity of fatality. The "Nocturne of Los Angeles" is one of the Mexican's few overtly sensual poems, and the angels have nothing in common with Rilke's angels of the *Duino Elegies*, who, although their role is ambiguous and variable, are close to the Dioscuri, "existential fullness, a goad to human striving but at the same time a measure of human insufficiency."²⁴ Or as Rilke himself said in a letter, "the Angel of the Elegies is the creature in whom that transformation of the visible with the invisible we are performing already appears complete. . . ."²⁵ Indeed, although Rilke's work may have been known to Villaurrutia and may have contributed in some way to the development of the Mexican's attitude toward death, Rilke's nearly mystical exaltation and his search for a non-Christian doctrine which would answer the riddle of immortality have little, if anything, in common with Villaurrutia's anguished groping in a world without answers, and any contact between the two is slight indeed.

There is, however, a much more likely source for some, at least, of both the symbols and the preoccupations which make Villaurrutia's poety so distinctly personal. Elías Nandino has commented that one of his friend's favorite works was Jean Cocteau's *Orphée*;²⁶ further, we know that Villaurrutia acted in

the Ulises production of the play in 1928. There are too many
interesting similarities for them to have been entirely coincidental. *Orphée* is very close to being a dramatic meditation on
death; Carl Wildman calls it a vision of "familiar things seen
in a new light . . .,"[27] and this would be a singularly apt description of much of the Mexican's work. Further, in Cocteau's
play, Death is a beautiful woman who dons surgical garb in
order to perform the magical ritual, and she and her assistants
pass through a mirror on their voyage between this world
and Death. We even have Cocteau's comment that Death loves
Orphée.[28] These are all familiar aspects of Villaurrutia's work:
mirrors abound—one, significantly, is the entranceway to Death
—a personalized Death was courted by Villaurrutia and even
became the object of love poetry, and his constant usage of
medical and technical terminology has been noted repeatedly.
There is here an interesting note; Nandino, a noted surgeon
as well as poet, has told this writer that Villaurrutia's medical
terminology was the result of a deep interest, and that he
frequently observed surgical operations. How this is related to
the fact of Cocteau's Death dressing in surgical garb is unclear.

Further, there is a clear antecedent of one of the Mexican
poet's most insistent themes in Heurtibise's speeches, such as
the following: "You have only to watch yourself all your life
in a mirror and you'll see Death at work like bees in a glass."[29]
Margaret Crosland has commented that *Orphée* is "the play
which is the key to the whole of Cocteau's attempt to explain
the nature of man and poet and his belief that life is only a
short space of time between one death and the next.[30] It is
obvious that Villaurrutia was deeply influenced by what he
perceived in Cocteau's play and that this influence helped form
his whole later poetic consciousness.

Both Nandino and Chumacero have referred to Jules Super-
vieille as the major poetic influence on their friend. Nandino
affirms that it was from Supervielle that Villaurrutia learned
"the trembling, the silent scream and the perception of the
ancestral sap in the burning branch of our blood. . . ."[31]
Chumacero goes so far as to state that one of the Mexican's
most important poems, "Nocturne of the Statue," is virtually
a paraphrase of Supervielle's "Saisir" (1928).[32] Certainly, the first

verse of "Saisir" is undoubtedly the model for Villaurrutia's poem:

Saisir:
To seize, to seize the evening, the apple and the statue,
to seize the shadow and the wall and the end of the street
To seize the foot, the neck of the sleeping woman
and then open the hands, filled with lost birds.
So many lost birds which become the street,
The statue, the wall, the evening, the apple and the statue.[33]

> Nocturne of the Statue:
> To dream, to dream the night, the street, the stairway
> and the scream of the statue turning the corner.
> To run toward the statue and find only the scream,
> to wish to touch the scream and find only the echo,
> to wish to touch the echo and find only the wall
> and to run toward the wall and touch a mirror.[34]

However, aside from the similarity of vocabulary and the obvious coincidence of the basic image, "Nocturne of the Statue" develops in a very different way from the remainder of "Saisir," which has none of the intense concentration of the nocturne.

There are similarities between some aspects of other poems of Supervielle and Villaurrutia's work; *Gravitation* (1925) abounds in walls, and in "Les yeux de la morte" Death is a woman. There is also an interesting emphasis on the human body in almost medical terms. Claude Roy has pointed out, "That heart whose dull, atrocious caprices, cruel intermittences inclines Supervielle's attention toward the enigma of his own body."[35] Roy is referring to the fact of Supervielle's cardiac condition, and attributes to it the emphasis on death and the body in Supervielle's poetry. This brings up the question of whether Villaurrutia knowingly suffered from a similar condition. If he were aware of the illness, it might well explain, at least in part, the stress on anguish and death, as well as the considerable use of biological imagery. Almost none of the critics accept this awareness, except for Rafael Solana, a friend who hints at it in one eulogistic article.[36] Further, Villaurrutia's close friend and personal physician, Dr. Elías Nandino, has stated to this writer that Villaurrutia had no history of cardiac

illness, which would seem to put an end to speculation. And
yet, so much of Villaurrutia's work leads to exactly this sort
of speculation; his poems are rich in biological imagery, including the heart, and *Queen of Hearts,* as we have seen, contains
overt hints that it is at least in part autobiographical, and there
is a specific reference to Villaurrutia himself which might well
be understood as an allusion to such an illness.

In any event, there is a clear source in Supervielle for the
"Nocturne of the Statue," and a strong similarity in vocabulary. Yet, there are marked differences between the two. The
French poet's work is full of the dead, in contrast to Villaurrutia, and in Supervielle there is no cosmic horror such as we
find in Villaurrutia's ambivalent attraction—dread toward final
extinction. And for Villaurrutia, it is very close to that, final
extinction of the individual, a return to the nameless from
which we spring. Even the watered-down immortality of Supervielle's "The only immortality of the dead is that which they
are granted by the fidelity of mortals . . ."[37] is far stronger than
Villaurrutia's attitude. Indeed, with the exception of a few
very early conventional religious mentions, questions of immortality as such are nonexistent in his work.

The Mexican's themes and production were much more restricted. There is nothing in his work comparable to Supervielle's landscape, his fascination for the theme of birth and
creation, or the poems of love and family, of kinship with the
beasts, and so on. More important, Dorothy Blair says of Supervielle's poetry of the period of "Saisir," "by the frailty of his own
body he is a prisoner condemned to death. By a closer understanding of his jailer, the body, and of his destiny, death, and
a closer contact with his future comrades, the dead, he can over-
come the fears with which he is assailed, so that in these poems
he seeks to enter into communion with himself, with his dead
parents, and then with the dead of all the ages."[38] In this way,
Supervielle hopes to exorcise his fear: "the final gift to man
is Death with hope. Death becomes a mercy and a liberation,
a cure for all the suffering of the flesh."[39] It is obvious that
this is not Villaurrutia's death, which was neither a merciful
liberation nor a door to the community of the dead, but part
of himself, of his personal consciousness. Villaurrutia neither
attempts to commune with the dead, nor does he even seem

to be conscious of this aspect of the problem. Whatever else, he is totally and eternally alone. From all the above, it is clear that Villaurrutia must have known Supervielle's work well and was undoubtedly influenced by it in the development of his poetic vocabulary and possibly in some of his themes, but it is equally clear that the point where he was not significantly influenced is that which has been often referred to as the most significant, the development of a *personal* death.

A related problem and one of the most difficult in a study of the poetry of Xavier Villaurrutia is the question of its Mexicanism. He was attacked savagely for refusing to consider poetry as a form of political propaganda, and certainly his work is not what some would expect of Mexican poetry. Braulio Sánchez-Sáez delightfully satirizes these pseudocritics and their idea that "in order to be a poet of Mexico it is necessary [to wear] a big Texas hat, a pair of good pistols, a sarape with flowered arabesques and mongoloid moustaches. . . ."[40] The question of Mexicanism in form is ridiculous; meter and rhythm recognize no national boundaries. The question of the Mexicanism of the content is, however, a legitimate one. The theme which will be developed here is much too extensive to be discussed exhaustively; we will treat it only insofar as it sheds light on the sources of Villaurrutia's work.[41]

Pedro Henríquez Ureña states in his *History of Culture in Hispanic America (Historia de la cultura en la América Hispánica)* that the baroque in Latin American architecture and plastic arts differs from the European variety, particularly in Mexico.[42] This unique quality of Mexican art and architecture becomes more marked as we enter the twentieth century and reaches complete fruition in the work of the great muralists, in painting, and such architectural marvels as the new Ciudad Universitaria, where at least part of the uniqueness is clearly due to an indigenous influence.

This same difference is apparent in the Mexican himself, particulary the man of the plateau, the Valley of Anahuac. Mexican gravity and courtesy are proverbial, and in his *Seis ensayos en busca de nuestra expresión* (Six Essays in Search of Our Expression), Henríquez Ureña explains the remarkable difference between the work of Juan Ruiz de Alarcón and that of the other giants of the Spanish Golden Age by Alarcón's Mexican

origin. (This is a highly debated question, and the bibliography
is extensive. For our purposes, however, the simple fact that a
critic as perceptive as Henríquez Ureña saw fit to study the
problem indicates the extent of this characteristic of Mexico.)

What is there in the cultural complex of Mexico which might
account for this peculiar shading? Anyone familiar with the
remnants of indigenous poetry which have been preserved has
noted the fact that two of its major themes are an absorption in
approaching death and a grave melancholy. Following are some
examples, taken from one of Angel María Garibay K.'s antholo-
gies of Indian poetry, *Poesía indígena de la altiplanicie*.[43] Adul-
terated as they may be, they can be considered representative.
The following excerpts are from *Canto de tristeza* (Song of
Sadness):

> I weep and am afflicted, when I remember
> that we will leave the lovely flowers,
>   the lovely songs:
> Let us be gay, let us sing: we all depart
>   and are lost.[44]

> Because my friends do not understand it thus,
> my heart is sorrowful and angered:
> they will not be engendered a second time,
> they will not be made children a second time,
> and they are already about to leave the earth.[45]

An atmosphere of sadness predominates, with an occasional note
of piercing agony as a poet speaks of imminent death.

One of the most remarkable poems in the collection is the
Concurso de poetas en casa de Tecayehuatzin (Contest of poets
in the House of Tecayehuatzin). This is a poetic disputation
in which the contestants alternate in singing of their realization
that life is ephemeral.

> Your heart knows it: only once
> have we come to live![46]

Frequently a line might be mistaken for a fragment of a
Nocturno.

> I do but suffer, because only
> in anguish do we live.[47]
> *Song of Orphanhood*

> Never in truth will it cease, never in truth
> will it go,
> nor will it become bearable, this sadness
> which now I express.[48]
> *Song in Praise of the Kings*

> We only come to sleep, we only come
> to dream:
> it is not true, it is not true that we come
> to live on the earth.[49]
> *Life Ephemeral*

This poetry is primarily concerned with death as the moment of passing into the afterlife, although it shows more interest in the fact of death itself than does Spanish poetry. The Indian was less certain about the existence and nature of the afterlife, and frequently turned to an attitude which might be called hedonistic masochism. Villaurrutia is closer to the Indian attitude than to the Spanish, although he chooses an intellectual solution which is diametrically opposed to their hedonism.

These references are not merely part of a poetic convention. The religious practice of human sacrifice was rooted in the belief that the gods had suffered as they created and therefore man should suffer in his turn in honor of the gods and to restore their vitality. "The idea of sacrifice expresses how life is nurtured permanently by death."[50] Mariano Picón-Salas speaks of the "cosmic horror of the Aztec"[51] and remarks that one of the psychological characteristics of the Indians which most impressed the conquerors was their sadness.

These examples show that the poetry of anguish and death has deep-rooted antecedents in the life and art of the pre-Conquest cultures of Anahuac. This indigenous tradition was crossed with the Spanish strain which had produced the *Coplas* of Jorge Manrique and which was to produce the acid poetry of death of Quevedo. It should come as no surprise if the fusion of these two cultural strains were to produce a synthesis which

also demonstrates this preoccupation, and if this is true, Villaurrutia's poetry is clearly rooted in the very sources of his
national culture.

Such a synthetic expression exists. Mexico is a land, as we
have seen, noted for its people's courteous gravity and reflective
seriousness. The theme of death is a constant in Mexican literature, almost dormant at times, but becoming in the twentieth
century a major preoccupation. It is a constant in the plastic
arts, from the stylized representations of pre-Conquest sculpture
to the inherent horror in the painting of Orozco, Siqueiros,
and Rivera. The work of such engravers as Posada at the turn
of the century is adequate testimony of the extent to which
death permeates the Mexican consciousness. Ricardo Ledesma
feels that the originality of Mexican poetry is precisely due to
the persistence of the Indian tradition of melancholy and
death,[52] and Juan M. Lope Blanch has found the insistence on
death in popular culture so great that he has devoted a philo-
logical study to the corresponding vocabulary; in it he quoted
Paul Westheim to the effect that Death "appears as a good
friend or a 'pal' with whom we permit ourselves to have a little
joke."[53] Even as conservative a writer as the Catholic novelist
Federico Gamboa demonstrates these attitudes, in his famous
Santa: "the death which we bear with us without bearing it, the
death which accompanies us everywhere without our notic-
ing. . . ."[54]

Villaurrutia himself was conscious of the *medio tono,* the
gravity and sobriety which so many critics have found as a
constant of Mexican poetry, and repeatedly commented on it. In
Young Mexican Poetry, he stated: "The work of the colonist Ruiz
de Alarcón has served to indicate, with some success, the character of our poetry, its qualities of sobriety, its crepuscular
half-tone. (That insistent, monotonous half-tone which weighs
on our lyric poetry and which even seems a mold chosen a
priori. . . .)"[55] Although Villaurrutia was referring to his own
generation and obviously felt that he was included among
those who were destined to assassinate the sobriety of Mexican
poetry, in his later work he clearly took his place within the
pattern. In comments published five days after his death,
Villaurrutia repeated this belief: "The characteristics of Mexican poetry of this half-century are the same characteristics of
the typical Mexican who is, by essence, reflexive, introverted,

circumspect and inner-directed. Therefore, Mexican poetry has that smooth and melodious half-tone."[56] It should be noted that he was referring quite specifically to twentieth-century Mexican poetry, in which he knew himself to be a major figure, and that this time, contrary to the discussion in *Young Mexican Poetry,* there were no expressions of any wish to change the form or any belief that he had done so.

In a lecture given in 1942, Villaurrutia listed what he considered to be the characteristics of Mexican poetry, which he saw as a continuum; cultivated, rather than popular, character; intimate lyricism; reflection and meditation; subtlety and wit; love for form; a "pearly gray" color; a crepuscular tonè; melancholy, a silent and withdrawn weeping; a delicate, muffled musicality; and finally, the insistence on death. These are, quite obviously, characteristics which in the large part we find in Villaurrutia's own work. He further states, "The Mexican is by nature silent. No little of the Indian which we bear within us influences these pauses and these silences of the Mexican, who, if he does not know how to speak very well, on the other hand, knows how to be silent excellently. Mexican lyricism is like the character of the Mexican, introverted, turned toward his interior abyss, toward his interior world."[57] It is perfectly obvious that Villaurrutia was acutely aware of his tradition and of the fact that this tradition springs from ancient sources; further, he must have been aware that he was describing his own work.

Nor is Villaurrutia the only member of his generation to have commented on these characteristics of Mexican poetry. In his *Perspective of Contemporary Mexican Literature (Perspectiva de la literatura mexicana actual.* 1915-1928. México, Contemporáneos, 1928), Jaime Torres Bodet remarks on the sober tone of the speech and dress of the highland Mexican (p. 14) and lists the qualities of Mexican literature much as did Villaurrutia: sobriety, a "delicate equilibrium of thought with form, of the idea and the sentence, of the substance and the profile."[58] Even a critic as hostile to the Contemporáneos as Raúl Leiva, has seen the indigenous heritage in Villaurrutia's work. "Xavier Villaurrutia was accused of being Europeanizing, when, if he was so, it was only on the periphery; within, in the depths, in the transcendental of his poetic message throbbed—invisible but present—the broad indigenous world with its nostalgia, with its dissatisfaction, with its very Mexican content of death. In spite of the European appearance, the accent, the real tone of his voice possesses notes which in the moments of greatest exaltation, of deepest surrender, of creative delirium, sounds with the voice of mixed blood, of conflict; the Indian drum and the cathedral organ from beyond the Atlantic are mixed, are fused and create a *new* voice, a different music."[59]

The other side of Villaurrutia's poetic theme, the problem of solipsism, can be attributed at least partially to the same elements in his heritage which contributed so much to his insistence on death. The stoic gravity of the Indian and the individualistic stoicism of the Spaniard are part of the tradition which has created those aspects of the Mexican personality which have already been discussed.

Octavio Paz, in his extraordinarily interesting study of Mexican life, customs and psychology, *El laberinto de la soledad* (The Labyrinth of Solitude), studies this aspect of Mexico in great detail, and stresses repeatedly the solitary nature of the Mexican, his cosmic loss of roots in his world, his familiarity with death and intimate treatment of it as a basic characteristic. He singles out Villaurrutia and the splendid poet José Gorostiza as representatives of the second of the two attitudes toward death which he finds permeating the Mexican consciousness: "Thus, there are two attitudes toward death: one, pointing forward, that conceives of it as creation; the other, pointing backward, that expresses itself as a fascination with nothingness or as a nostalgia for limbo."[60]

It should not perhaps be given too much weight, but there is a typically Villaurrutian ironic hint of his own awareness of his cultural roots in the fact that the definitive edition of *Nostalgia of Death* was published by Editorial Mictlán, Mictlán being the Aztec land of the dead, a nebulous zone to which the departed repaired and whose ultimate stopping place was left very much in question. It seems clear that whatever the final source for Villaurrutia's personal concept of death, whether in Cocteau or some other source or in a deliberate elaboration of an original concept, Villaurrutia himself, despite the charges of anti-Mexicanism, was rooted firmly in the tradition of his people and his nation, and his poetry must, in order to be understood properly, be regarded as a fusion of these two traditions.

CHAPTER 5

A Summing-Up

Xavier Villaurrutia's impact on Mexican literature was a decisive one. Although it would be difficult to characterize anyone as a disciple of his, Villaurrutia's unmistakable tone speaks from the pages of many writers. Edmundo Báez, better known for his work in other genres, shows a clear influence in such poems as "Letter to a Poet,"[1] and Rafael Solana attributed to Villaurrutia a decisive influence on the poetess Guadalupe Amor and the poets Neftalí Beltrán and Elías Nandino.[2] Certainly he speaks clearly in the early work of Alí Chumacero, and Villaurrutia's personal brand of mocking wit has deeply influenced the playwright Emilio Carballido, among others. But to equate influence with the number of echoes in younger authors is a grave misunderstanding. Whether Villaurrutia's work had ever directly influenced other works or not, his impact on Mexican letters would have been of major importance because of what his highly conscious art represented. The lesson of craftsmanship, of professionalism in the very highest sense of the word, are his most important legacy in these terms. His consciousness that each poem was an act requiring the highest concentration of intellectual and creative powers, his disdain for facile creation and rejection of the cliché and the commonplace, have been a lesson of conscience, which his friends have acknowledged freely. The magnetic, enigmatic personality which enabled him to be at the center of so many literary groups, attracted younger writers to him for guidance. Rodolfo Usigli has emphasized this debt in saying, "he had an indefatigable curiosity, an inexhaustable talent, and one of his greatest pleasures was to work with other writers, making them see the errors into which they had fallen or the manner in which they could improve what they had written."[3] Usigli goes on to point out the novels,

123

plays and poetry of Rafael Solana, the poetry of Octavio Paz, the plays of Agustín Lazo, and his own dramatic works as specific examples of revisions at Villaurrutia's suggestion. Lùis Basurto reflects the same gratitude when he says, "he was, above all, a generous animator who stimulated vocations in the class-room, on the stage, in the daily contact of his privileged friend-ship. . . ."[4] Basurto indicates the extent to which he feels Villaurrutia was a vital influence, transcending the confines of direct stylistic or thematic contact, when he states, "How many writers, directors, incipient authors, found the exact phrase of self-criticism and of orientation on his lips. . . ."[5] The same rigorous perfectionism which has made Villaurrutia's criticism a model of its kind, which made his study the key step in the radical re-evaluation of López Velarde's work, extended to the help offered to other artists.

Obviously, Villaurrutia's historical importance must not be underestimated. Without his genius for welding varied artistic talents and temperaments into a productive group, the growth of the theater in Mexico would have been retarded considerably. His historical importance is not, however, an estimate of his worth as a playwright. It is difficult to estimate the worth of any single author relative to his ambient, more difficult still to make absolute judgments, regardless of particular cir-cumstances. In this case, however, there can be no question of his merit relative to other Mexican playwrights. With Rodolfo Usigli, he stands far above other Mexican dramatists of his time. Whether he or Usigli is the better playwright is a moot question, open to personal preferences.

The problems with which Villaurrutia deals are universal, although it would be a grave error to regard him as not firmly rooted in his tradition. Giuseppe Bellini points out in his splen-did study of Villaurrutia's theater that it functions on a high level of universality but always in terms of his heritage. "His process does not mean the reduction of problems from univer-sality to regional limitations, but the elevation from a geo-graphically determined world to universality."[6] He was a student of the human soul in torment. Although this torment shows certain similarities from one play to another, the themes and perspectives are sufficiently varied to prevent the criticism that he had only one string to his bow.

It is perfectly true that Villaurrutia's theater is rigidly controlled, which has led some to mistake this control for coldness. His characters all speak the same correct language, but it is a language which became in Villaurrutia's hands an edged instrument which extracted the most of meaning from a dramatic situation. To make the criticism that his dramas are not passionate is to confuse passion with rhetoric; beneath the scalpel which amuses as it cuts, human passion is revealed palpitating and ever more human.

It is, however, perhaps as a poet that Villaurrutia achieved his greatest work. The same search for truth which moves his theater lies at the heart of his dissection of his own spiritual dilemma, his own quest for impossible answers. He is the first Mexican poet to give expression to man's radical solitude in our torn century, to "define in Mexico the crisis of sensibility of the modern world, as the metaphysical poets of the early seventeenth century did in England. . . ."[7] If, as Chumacero has said, Villaurrutia succeeded in making the "complicated and singular world of his consciousness lasting in the history of Mexican literature as a lesson of personal rigor and an example of passionate vocation . . .,"[8] he also created a poetry whose expression of this complicated and singular world speaks to man everywhere.

Notes and References

Chapter One

1. *Pasado inmediato y otros ensayos*, México, 1941, p. 22.
2. See Antonio Magaña Esquivel, *Sueño y realidad del teatro*, México, 1949, p. 26.
3. *Obras*, p. 823.
4. "Si Enrique González Martínez era, hacia 1918, el dios mayor y casi único de nuestra poesía; si de él partían las inspiraciones, si los jóvenes cantaban con pulmones propios el dolor particular de González Martínez, en oraciones semejantes al tedioso orfeón que en torno de Dios deben entonar los ángeles, necesitamos nuevamente de Adán y Eva que vinieran a darnos con su rebelión, con su pecado, una tierra nuestra de más amplias panoramas, de mayores libertades, una tierra que ver con nuestros propios ojos. La fórmula será: Adán y Eva=Ramón López Velarde y José Juan Tablada." *Obras*, p. 825.
5. *El trato con escritores*, 1a. serie, México, 1961, p. 133.
6. "Autobiografía en tercera persona," *Revista de Bellas Artes*, 7 (enero-febrero 1966), 7.
7. Merlin Forster, "La fecha de nacimiento de Xavier Villaurrutia," *Rev. Iberoamericana*, XXXIII, 63 (enero-junio 1967), 131-32.
8. *Obras*, p. 575.
9. *Obras*, p. 583.
10. *Hoy*, 724 (6 enero 1951), 38.
11. *Obras*, p. 683.
12. ". . . los simbolistas franceses . . . dejaban su música, su atmósfera y no pocas veces sus palabras." *Obras*, p. 642.
13. *Perspectiva de la literatura mexicana actual, 1915-1928*, Mexico, 1928, p. 3.
14. "*Contemporáneos* and the Limits of Art," *Romance Notes*, V (1964), 2.
15. Villaurrutia, Cuesta, Gorostiza, and Ortiz de Montellano, *Una botella al mar*, México, 1946, p. 17.

16. *Hoy,* 628, marzo 5, 1949; quoted by Luis Leal, "Torres Bodet y los 'Contemporáneos,'" *Hispania,* XL, 3 (Sept. 1957), 292.

17. *Las revistas literarias de Hispanoamérica,* México, 1959, 99.

18. "Así me querrías, soberbio, alto, amante, dorado, capaz de vivir novelas frenéticas, capaz de escribir poesías más frenéticas aún. Te equivocas. Yo sufro porque no puedo complacerte. Imagino que no puedes pensar en mí tan contemporáneo de Xavier Villaurrutia, tan invisible como él, aspirante a diplomático, negligente en el vestir; con un cuerpo inclinado cada día más a desaparecer entre los millones de jóvenes . . . con mis trajes holgados, con mis camisas blandas, con mis movimientos de cabeza que acompañan al jazz . . . con mis cigarrillos mojados en perfume, efímeros, perfectos. . . . Quiéreme así, frívolo, alegre, con mi concepto de la vida y del arte como un deporte distinguido y nada más" *Obras,* p. 582.

19. "Presencia de Villaurrutia," *Revista de Guatemala,* 2a. época, I, 1 (abril-junio 1951), 190.

20. *Obras,* p. 737.

21. *Obras,* p. 736.

22. *Obras,* p. 736.

23. Magaña Esquivel, *Imagen del teatro,* México, 1940, p. 83.

24. Lazo, "Presencia de Villaurrutia," p. 190.

Chapter Two

1. "A mí no me es posible decir: ¡Voy a ponerme a escribir!, es preciso abandonarme por largo tiempo en el que voy madurando, cristalizando . . . una idea, hasta que llega un momento sobre el que no tengo ningún mandato y puedo decirme: ¡Ahora *sé* que voy a escribir! Es decir, escribo *inevitablemente,* ¡esa es la palabra exacta!" Quoted by José Luis Martínez, "Con Xavier Villaurrutia," *Tierra Nueva* (marzo-abril, 1940), 77.

2. "Juego difícil, de ironía y de inteligencia." Quoted by Chumacero, *Obras,* p. xi.

3. "Para mí no tiene sentido alguno la poesía que es puro juego exterior o encanto de los sentidos. La musicalidad de una estrofa, la belleza de ciertas palabras, no me llama en lo absoluto cuando se busca como intención de la poesía." Martínez, "Con Xavier Villaurrutia," p. 76.

4. ". . . si existe un goce sentimental o emotivo, ¿por qué no puede haber un goce de la idea?" *Ibid.,* pp. 76-77.

5. ". . . puede construirse con ideas la poesía, siempre que éstas se den en función de vida y preocupación auténticas." *Ibid.,* p. 80.

6. *Obras,* xiv.

7. "Dulzura hay en el alma, y juventud, y vida,/ y perfume en la tarde . . .," "Tarde."

8. "Una humilde verdad como descanso,/ un silencio apacible, un libro amado . . .," "La bondad de la vida."

9. ". . . en el claroscuro envejecido/ de un melancólico retrato. . . ."

10. *Rasgos*, México, 1943, p. 130.

11. "La poesía de Xavier Villaurrutia," *Memoria del Segundo Congreso Internacional de Catedráticos de Literatura Iberoamericana*, Los Angeles, 1940.

12. ". . . para que el domingo/ fuera detrás del tren/ persiguiéndome . . .," "Domingo."

13. ". . . nos ha estrujado,/ inútiles, en los rincones," "Fonógrafos."

14. Y el silencio se mueve
y vibra
en torno de la llama blanda,
como el ala—¿de qué presagio?,
¿de qué insecto?—que acaricia,
que enfría, que empequeñece.

15. La soledad se agranda
como las sombras
en la sábana del muro,
como las caras de ayer. . . .

16. *Obras*, xviii.

17. "La noche juega con los ruidos/ copiándolos en sus espejos/ de sonidos."

18. "Lenta y morada/ pone ojeras en los cristales/ y en la mirada."

19. ". . . Corren locas/ de incendio, huyendo/ de sí mismas,/ entre los esqueletos de las otras/ inmóviles. . . ."

20. Vámonos inmóviles de viaje
para ver la tarde de siempre
con otra mirada,
para ver la mirada de siempre
con distinta tarde.

Vámonos, inmóviles.

21. Y el corazón,
el corazón de mica
—sin diástole ni sístole—
enloquece bajo la aguja
y sangra en gritos su pasado.

22. ". . . el metal de los reflejos . . .," "Reflejos."

23. ". . . el metal de los instantes . . .," "Reloj."

24. ". . . este polvo blanco . . .," "Noche."

25. ". . . caracol de los oídos. . . ."

26. ". . . ecos de plata de agua. . . ."

27. ". . . la placa de mi retina," "Lugares-III."

130

XAVIER VILLAURRUTIA

28. ". . . lleno de dorado calor/ se hiela . . .," "Interior."
29. ". . . que no tenga sabor . . .," "Interior."
30. *Antología de la poesía mexicana,* México, 1928, p. 20.
31. Introductory note to *Décima muerte y otros poemas no coleccionados.*
32. "Eres la compañía con quien hablo/ de pronto, a solas."
33. "Las palabras que salen del silencio. . . ."
34. "Tanque de sueño en que me ahogo/ libre hasta despertar."
35. Tu mano metálica
endurece la prisa de mi mano
y conduce la pluma
que traza en el papel su litoral.
36. See Enrique González Rojo, "Dama de Corazones," *Contemporáneos,* I, 3 (agosto 1928), 320.
37. "El texto de *Dama de corazones* no pretende ser el de una novela ni alcanzar nada más de lo que me propuse que fuera: un monólogo interior en que seguía la consciencia de un personaje durante un tiempo real preciso, y durante un tiempo psíquico condicionado por las reflexiones conscientes, por las emociones y por los sueños reales o inventados del protagonista que, a pesar de expresarse en primera persona, no es necesariamente yo mismo. . . . *Dama de corazones* pretendía, a la vez, ser un ejercicio de prosa dinámica, erizada de metáforas, ágil y ligera, como la que, como una imagen del tiempo en que fue escrita, cultivaban Giraudoux o, más modestamente, Pierre Girard." "El relato. *Dama de corazones.* La novela," *Revista de Bellas Artes,* 7 (enero-febrero 1966), 19-20.
38. See Rafael Solana, "Villaurrutia, prosista," *Hoy,* 725 (13 enero 1951), 46-47.
39. . . . miro el cuarto de estudio tapizado de un verde sombrío. *Obras,* p. 573.
40. La luz . . . se tamiza suavemente en los cristales y en las cortinas de ligera cretona. *Obras,* p. 574.
41. . . . un día espléndido que habrás de partir y gustar como el fruto maduro. . . . *Obras,* p. 579.
42. . . . ese túnel de agua de los años, que puede al fin ahogarte. . . . *Obras,* p. 582.
43. El ruido de mis pasos me sale al encuentro rechazado por los muros. *Obras,* p. 591.
44. No es difícil morir. Yo había muerto ya, en vida, algunas veces. Todo estriba en no hacer un solo movimiento, en no decir una sola palabra, en fijar los ojos en un punto, cerca, lejos. Sobre todo, en no distraerse en mil cosas. *Obras,* pp. 585-86.
45. Morir equivale a estar desnudo, sobre un diván de hielo, en un día de calor, con los pensamientos dirigidos a un solo blanco que

no gira como el blanco de los tiradores ingenuos que pierden su fortuna en las ferias. Morir es estar incomunicado felizmente de las personas y las cosas, y mirarlas como la lente de la cámara debe mirar, con exactitud y frialdad. Morir no es otra cosa que convertirse en un ojo perfecto que mira sin emocionarse. *Obras,* p. 586.

46. "Cultura de la muerte," *Sur,* año VIII, 47 (agosto 1938), 82.

47. ¿Y quién entre las sombras de una calle desierta
en el muro, lívido espejo de soledad,
no se ha visto pasar o venir a su encuentro
y no ha sentido miedo, angustia, duda mortal?
El miedo de no ser sino un cuerpo vacío
que alguien, yo mismo o cualquier otro, puede ocupar,
y la angustia de verse fuera de sí, viviendo,
y la duda de ser o no ser realidad.
(Nocturno miedo.)

48. ¿Será mía aquella sombra
sin cuerpo que va pasando?
¿Y mía la voz perdida
que va la calle incendiando?

49. Soledad, aburrimiento,
vano silencio profundo,
líquida sombra en que me hundo,
vacío del pensamiento.

50. ". . . este naufragio invisible."

51. ". . . o la que así llamamos inútilmente. . . ."

52. . . . porque vida silencio piel y boca
y soledad recuerdo cielo y humo
nada son sino sombras de palabras
que nos salen al paso de la noche.

53. Al fin llegó la noche a despertar palabras
ajenas, desusadas, propias, desvanecidas. . . .

54. El más ligero ruido crece de pronto y, luego, muere sin agonía.

55. Y es inútil que encienda a mi lado una lámpara:
la luz hace más honda la mina del silencio
y por ella desciendo, inmóvil, de mí mismo.

56. . . . . mar de un sueño antiguo,
de un sueño hueco y frío en el que ya no queda
del mar sino los restos de un naufragio de olvidos.

57. Porque la noche arrastra en su baja marea
memorias angustiosas, temores congelados,
la sed de algo que, trémulos, apuramos un día,
y la amargura de lo que ya no recordamos.

58. ". . . el mar antiguo edipo. . . ."

59. Lo llevo en mí como un remordimiento,
pecado ajeno y sueño misterioso,
y lo arrullo y lo duermo
y lo escondo y lo cuido y le guardo el secreto.

60. . . . junto a tu cuerpo más muerto que muerto
que no es tu cuerpo ya sino su hueco. . . .

61. ". . . la estatua que despierta/ en la alcoba de un mundo que ha muerto."

62. ". . . más que solos y náufragos,/ todavía más, y cada vez más, todavía."

63. "Ciudad sumergida. . . ."

64. ¡Y dudo! Y no me atrevo a preguntarme si es
el despertar de un sueño o es un sueño mi vida.

65. Miedo de no ser nada más que un jirón del sueño
de alguien—¿de Dios?—que sueña en este mundo amargo.
Miedo de que despierte ese alguien—¿Dios?—el dueño
de un sueño cada vez más profundo y más largo.

66. "¡ . . . polvo en el polvo y olvido en el olvido!"

67. Pero alguien, en la angustia de una noche vacía,
· sin saberlo él, ni yo, alguien que no ha nacido
dirá con mis palabras su nocturna agonía.

68. "Estoy muerta de sueño."

69. ". . . cotidiana muerte provisional . . .," *Obras*, p. 684.

70. "Estatua sin sangre. . . ."

71. Sin gota de sangre
sin ruido ni peso
a mis pies clavados
vino a dar mi cuerpo.

Lo tomé en los brazos
lo llevé a mi lecho.
Cerraba las alas
profundas el sueño.

72. ". . . escondida en un hueco de mi ropa en la maleta,/ en el bolsillo de uno de mis trajes,/ entre las páginas de un libro. . . ."

73. . . . Aquí estoy.
Te he seguido como la sombra
que no es posible dejar así no más en casa;
como un poco de aire cálido e invisible
mezclado al aire duro y frío que respiras;
como el recuerdo de lo que más quieres. . . .

74. ". . . sueño en que quisieras creer que vives/ sin mí, cuando yo misma lo dibujo y lo borro. . . ."

75. "Aquí estoy, ¿no me sientes?/ Abre los ojos; ciérralos, si quieres."

76. "La poesía de Xavier Villaurrutia," *Estaciones,* Invierno 1956, p. 26.

77. "Estética de la muerte," *El Universal* (3 nov. 1938), 3.

78. "El hombre actual muere y asiste—al menos yo asisto—a su propia muerte. Y . . . a la de los demás. El *memento mori* y el *arte de morir* son para mí de una angustiosa actualidad." "Contestación a la encuesta de *Romance,*" *Romance,* I, 4 (15 marzo 1940), 2.

79. "La muerte no es, para mí, ni fin, ni un puente tendido hacia otra vida, sino una constante presencia, un vivirla y palparla segundo a segundo . . . presencia que sorprende en el placer y en el dolor." Martínez, "Con Xavier Villaurrutia," 77.

80. "La muerte no es, para mí, sólo el término de la vida. El vivir para disponerse a bien morir o simplemente morir me parecen verdades de las que una verdad más profunda queda justificadamente ausente. Tampoco me satisface considerar la vida como una prisión de la que salimos, al fin, gracias a la muerte. Mi poesía es la presencia de la muerte durante toda la vida, ya que el hombre vive su propia muerte." Letter to Alfredo Cardona Peña, quoted in *Semblanzas mexicanas,* México, 1955, p. 150.

81. ". . . en momentos como los que ahora vivimos, la muerte és lo único que no le pueden quitar al hombre; le pueden quitar la fortuna, la vida, la ilusion, pero la muerte, ¿quién me la a quitar? Si la muerte la llevamos, como decía un poeta, dentro, como el fruto lleva la semilla. Nos acompaña siempre, desde el nacimiento, y nuestra muerte crece con nosotros. La muerte es también una patria a la que se vuelve; por eso es posible que haya un libro de versos que se llama *Nostalgia de la muerte.* Nostalgia de lo ya conocido. La muerte es algo ya conocido por el hombre." "La poesía," *Revista de Bellas Artes,* 7 (enero-feb. 1966), 18.

82. En diversas salas de espera
    aguardan la misma muerte
    los pasajeros de color
    y los blancos, de primera.

83. . . . algo de dulce sueño,
    de sueño sin angustia,
    infantil, tierno, leve
    goce no recordado. . . .

84. ". . . caída de un silencio sobre otro/ y de la blanca persistencia del olvido. . . ."

85. Villaurrutia's use of the term "nocturne" for many of his poems does not correspond to any particular formal structure or thematic mode; many of his poems which bear other titles could just as well

have been called nocturnes. Why he chose to call this particular section "Nostalgias" is difficult to determine, except that all but "Death in Tenths" are marked by a non-Mexican geographical setting: North Carolina, snow.

86. Cuando he perdido toda fe en el milagro . . .
    . . . cuando el cielo de invierno no es más que la ceniza
    de algo que ardió hace muchos siglos . . .
    . . . cuando me encuentro tan solo, tan solo . . .
    . . . cuando cierro los ojos pensando inútilmente . . .
87. ". . . el infierno frío, . . . el eterno invierno. . . ."
88. . . . me encuentro tan sólo, tan sólo,
    que me busco en mi cuarto
    como se busca, a veces, un objeto perdido,
    una carta estrujada en los rincones. . . .
89. Siento que estoy viviendo aquí mi muerte,
    mi sola muerte presente,
    mi muerte que no puedo compartir ni llorar,
    mi muerte de que no me consolaré jamás.
90. ". . . mi linfa y mi carne estremecidas. . . ."
91. . . . cómo el agua y la sangre
    son otra vez la misma agua marina,
    y cómo se hiela primero
    y luego se vuelve cristal
    y luego duro mármol,
    hasta inmovilizarme en el tiempo más angustioso y lento,
    con la vida secreta, muda e imperceptible
    del mineral, del tronco, de la estatua.
92. "Escribí las cinco restantes después de una involuntaria y larga pausa," *Décima muerte y otros poemas no coleccionados,* note.
93. Recently a number of critics have examined the use and scope of this and related techniques. See, for example, Dámaso Alonso, *Poesía española. Ensayo de métodos y límites estilísticos,* especially his chapter "Lope de Vega, símbolo del barroco."
94. ". . . en tierra, en polvo, en humo, en sombra, en nada."
95. ". . . es cadáver, es polvo, es sombra, es nada."
96. "Ven muerte tan escondida/ que no te sienta venir."
97. "tu cuerpo yerto."
98. ". . . será posible, acaso,/ vivir después de haber muerto."
99. ". . . te encuentro en el hueco/ de una forma. . . ."
100. ¿qué será, Muerte, de ti
     cuando al salir yo del mundo,
     deshecho el nudo profundo,
     tengas que salir de mí?
101. ". . . no hay hora en que yo no muera!"

102. "Lo plástico de su poesía se ajusta mejor al equilibrio de las formas, al dibujo de los objectos, a la calidad de la materia empleada, a la estática de las actitudes." *Antología de la poesía mexicana moderna*, p. 203.

103. ". . . poesía construida en función del tacto y la vista." *Ibid.*

104. ". . . dibuja con su mano/ de sombra . . . ," "Noche."

105. ". . . en un hueco de mi ropa en la maleta,/ en el bolsillo de uno de mis trajes,/ entre las páginas de un libro . . . ," "Nocturno en que habla la muerte."

106. ". . . tu silencio duro cristal de dura roca . . . ," "Nocturno mar."

107. ". . . ciudad sumergida . . . ," "Estancias nocturnas."

108. ". . . el mar de un sueño antiguo,/ de un sueño hueco y frío en el que ya no queda/ del mar sino los restos de un naufragio de olvidos," "Nocturno."

109. *La Palabra y el Hombre*, abril-junio, 1964. See also his "Correlación y paralelismo en la poesía de Xavier Villaurrutia," *La Palabra y el Hombre* (enero-marzo 1966), 81-90.

110. ". . . una pálida sonrisa de muerte juguetea en los labios del poeta." "Tres poetas mexicanos," *Revista Iberoamericana*, I, 1 (mayo 1939), 86.

111. "Villaurrutia desde aquí," *Nivel*, 36, 25 dic. 1961.

112. ". . . ejercicios que aunque ingeniosos, restan intensidad al poema . . . ," Berkeley-Los Angeles, 1953, p. 205.

113. "Nunca pondría en mi poesía una sola palabra sin un sentido exacto o bien que fuera puramente decorativa. Si he usado de los 'juegos de palabras' es porque han sido precisos para expresar con ellos alguna idea. Por otra parte, el 'juego de palabras' aparece ya en la poesía española—en Lope, por ejemplo—aunque no con la frecuencia con que existe en la poesía francesa y en la inglesa, donde es enteramente común." "La poesía," *Revista de Bellas Artes*, 7 (enero-febrero 1966), 18.

114. "Y en el juego angustioso de un espejo frente a otro/ cae mi voz. . . ."

115. ". . . un medio gráfico y sutil para representar el rebote angustioso de una voz caída entre el mutuo e infinito reflejo de un espejo frente a otro, reproducido una vez y otra vez, en su superficie, en diferentes matices representados por el juego de las palabras que conservan idénticos fonemas." "Con Xavier Villaurrutia," 79.

116. . . . aquí en el caracol de la oreja
    el latido de un mar en el que *no sé nada*
    en el que *no se nada*. . . .

117. La sonrisa del niño
que no comprende al mundo
y que lo encuentra hermoso:
¡del niño que no sabe todavía!

118. "... sin dejar otra huella/ que la que deja el ala/ de un pájaro en el viento."

119. *Obras*, p. xx.

120. "... una angustia, una pregunta,/ una suspensa y luminosa duda."

121. Amar es reconstruir, cuando te alejas,
tus pasos, tus silencios, tus palabras,
y pretender seguir tu pensamiento
cuando a mi lado, al fin inmóvil, callas.

122. Amar es no dormir cuando en mi lecho
sueñas entre mis brazos que te ciñen,
y odiar el sueño en que, bajo tu frente,
acaso en otros brazos te abandonas.

123. ... si nuestro amor no fuera
como un hilo tendido
en que vamos los dos
sin red sobre el vacío. ...

124. ... la sombría
caverna de mi agonía ...

125. ... y cuando a solas te invoco
en la oscura piedra toco
tu impasible compañía.

126. Mi amor por ti, ¡no murió!
sigue viviendo en la fría,
ignorada galería
que en mi corazón cavó.

127. Por el temor de quererme
tanto como yo te quiero,
has preferido, primero,
para salvarte, perderme.

128. ... ¿por qué, dolorosa y mustia,
no rompemos la angustia
para salir de la nada?

129. ... oigo tu voz en el eco
y hallo tu forma en el hueco
que has dejado en el vacío.

130. *Summa*, no. 1, julio 1953.

131. ... aunque fui tuyo, entre tus brazos frío,
tu calor y tu aliento fueron vanos:
cada vez más te siento menos mío.

132. Es inútil mi fiebre de alcanzarte,
mientras tú mismo que todo lo puedes
no vengas en mis redes a enredarte.

133. Volver a una patria lejana,
volver a una patria olvidada,
oscuramente deformada
por el destierro en esta tierra.
¡Salir del aire que me encierra!
Y anclar otra vez en la nada.
La noche es mi madre y mi hermana,
la nada es mi patria lejana,
la nada llena de silencio,
la nada llena de vacío,
la nada sin tiempo ni frío,
la nada en que no pasa nada.

134. Duerme aquí, silencioso e ignorado,
el que en vida vivió mil y una muertes.
Nada quieras saber de mi pasado.
Despertar es morir. ¡No me despiertes!

Chapter Three

1. Although Villaurrutia had written earlier works, he destroyed them; the only piece extant is *Dialogue (Diálogo)*, a debate between Education and Culture, of no real interest.

2. "Difíciles por su aparente sencillez las piezas en un acto equivalen, en un juego de retóricas comparadas, a formas tan concretas, sostenidas y peligrosas como el soneto. No hay mejor disciplina para un autor dramático que someterse a la prueba de las obras en un acto. . . . Tal vez por eso las escribí, y, seguramente, por eso les guardo un lúcido afecto."

3. ". . . el público ama el enigma; . . . no es preciso darle una única solución de él, cuando se ha logrado ponerlo en juego, intrigarlo, amenazarlo con el grito de la esfinge: 'Adivina o te devoro.' "

4. ". . . piense en que la comodidad y la ignorancia en que se desarrollaba su vida no era más que una realidad vacía, un mundo deshabitado, un camino sin paisaje, un sueño sin ensueños: en una palabra, una muerte eterna; y en que ahora, . . . gracias a una revelación, a la revelación de un secreto, se halla usted en el umbral de una existencia que podrá discutir, corregir y labrar a su antojo. . . ." *Obras*, p. 107.

5. "*¿En qué piensas?*" tiene, conscientemente, una apariencia de banalidad, pero la procesión va por dentro. Recuerdo que un cronista la acusaba de 'intrascendente,' pero en su crónica hablaba de Bergson, de las nociones del tiempo, del tiempo psíquico. No se daba cuenta

de que, precisamente, estaba poniendo el dedo en la llaga. . . ." "El teatro. Recuerdos y figuras," *Revista de Bellas Artes,* 7 (enero-febrero 1966), 15.

6. "Yo amo, simplemente. Amo a quien me ama." *Obras,* p. 125.

7. "Antonio y yo hemos buscado en esta ciudad, en esta casa, un objeto que hemos perdido. Hemos rastreado en todos los rincones, hemos encendido todas las luces, ¡No lo hemos encontrado! Y ahora, de mutuo acuerdo, vamos a buscar ese objeto en el único lugar donde estamos seguros de no hallarlo." *Obras,* p. 136.

8. ". . . he intentado todos los medios: hablo dormida y confieso faltas que no he cometido, le escribo anónimos diciéndole que le engaño, invito a cenar a los que fueron mis pretendientes. Un día, al ver llegar a Luis, abracé al chofer japonés. . . ." *Obras,* p. 133.

9. María Luisa: Cuando Carlos me amaba, como tú ahora, no sabías que ya me amabas, pero yo te amaba desde entonces, porque sabía que un día me amarías.

Carlos (*colérico*): Y ahora le ha tocado a Ramón su turno.

María Luisa: No me entiendes. . . . No es su turno, no. No es que esté detrás o después del otro en mi amor . . . yo te amo, no porque hayas dejado de amarme sino porque un día me amaste.

Víctor: Está bien ¿pero a mí?

María Luisa: A ti te amo, eso es todo.

Víctor: Luego Ramón sale sobrando.

Obras, p. 127.

10. "Prediquemos con el ejemplo." *Obras,* p. 154.

11. Napoleón: . . . será bueno que no olvidemos que entre las señoras presentes hay una señorita.

La Señorita (*avergonzada de seguir siéndolo*): Yo, señor.

Napoleón (*tras un rápido examen*): Nada más justo. *Obras,* p. 149.

12. "Pausa. Una misteriosa luz cenital invade el estudio. Todos permanecen inmóviles, abstraídos." *Obras,* p. 129.

13. ". . . una opaca luz de acuario." *Obras,* p. 109.

14. ". . . una aureola de luz sideral [que] brilla en torno de su cabeza. . . ." *Obras,* p. 161.

15. "La imitación servil, fotográfica, de los modelos exteriores y de los fragmentos de vida también exterior, han venido relegando al teatro a un lugar que no merece entre todas las artes.

"El autor dramático olvida, las más de las veces, que es un inventor, un creador, un poeta; y que la obra de teatro tiene el deber de objetivar y materializar, no aquello que de hecho ya está objetivado y materializado a los ojos de todos, sino aquello que aún no lo está y que, profundo y huidizo, merece estarlo.

"Acaso el camino del teatro actual no sea otro que una completa desrealización, un cambio radical de los medios escénicos, para llegar a captar más profundamente lo *real* interior y exterior del hombre.

"El teatro tiene su poesía privativa: en el lenguaje, en la acción, en la sorpresa; en la creación de lo que pudiéramos llamar la poesía de la acción. El teatro es, entre otras muchas cosas, plástica. Pero no sólo es plástica. También es arquitectura y también dicción, música, danza. Lo plástico es solo un medio teatral, pero no debe considerarse, nunca, claro, por si solo, como un fin."

"El teatro. Recuerdos y figuras," *Revista de Bellas Artes,* 7 (enero-feb. 1966), 15.

16. "Hace pensar . . . en el sepulturero convertido en agente de inhumaciones que Shakespeare pondría en su *Hamlet* si fuera contemporáneo nuestro." *Obras,* p. 592.

17. ". . . todo parece preparado para provocar el espionaje. Las paredes, tapizadas de un color azul pizarra; los muebles, tapizados de un verde sordo, a apagar las palabras mejor que a facilitar las conversaciones. Una puerta en el fondo comunica con el cuarto de Alberto; otra, a la izquierda, con el vestíbulo; dos a la derecha, con la biblioteca y la sala. Más que puertas son huecos totalmente disimulados por cortinas del mismo verde sordo de los muebles, llenas de pliegues para disimular las formas. Unos cuantos detalles más harían de esta antesala la cámara transmisora de una estación de radio; todo objeto que provoque resonancias ha sido cuidadosamente evitado, y hasta la luz, de tarde, parece, al filtrarse por muros y cortinas, expresarse en voz baja." *Obras,* p. 367.

18. "Y ahora aquí a tu lado, comprendo que todo fué como si mi sombra hubiera querido abandonar para siempre mi cuerpo echándose a buscar su destino, que no es el mío . . . porque el destino, eso que llamamos el destino, no está fuera de nosotros, en una ciudad, en una fecha, en una persona, sino dentro de nosotros, en el centro mismo de nosotros . . . y también ahora sé que ese destino no lo podemos dejar, abandonándolo, o renunciando a él, ni siquiera buscando la muerte, porque entonces, ¿quién nos dice que el suicidio no era precisamente nuestro destino?" *Obras,* 401.

19. ". . . yo estoy aquí en este ambiente, dentro de estas paredes, rodeado por estos muebles y por estos objetos que son la imagen o la compañía de la muerte, porque la muerte es mi elemento, como el agua al pez. Y dime, ¿quién va a pensar que el pez se halla preso en el agua? Querer salir a la vida, es en mi caso, una locura que me ahogaría. . . ." *Obras,* p. 402.

20. "Comprendo que por semanas enteras la abandono a una vida monótona, incolora, para seguir la mía con temor de romper la soledad que me envuelve. Comprendo que soy egoísta, frío y duro,

a veces, como un hombre de vidrio; pero, también como un hombre
de vidrio, si una respiración ajena me empaña, una sospecha, una
duda, me hacen trizas. Imagina el tiempo que necesito luego para
rehacerme en una cicatrización lenta, dolorosa, una cicatrización sin
sangre . . . en una cicatrización de linfático." *Obras*, p. 376.

21. *Teatro messicano del 900*, Milano, 1959, pp. 35-58.

22. *Ibid.*, p. 47.

23. "La agencia queda vacía. El silencio parece vibrar. La luz del
interior se hace opaca, lechosa, al tiempo que las luces de fuera se
intensifican. Sin que nada ni nadie la mueva, la cubierta del ataúd
del escaparate se cierra con un golpe breve y seco. La pausa es más
profunda. A través del cristal del escaparate se ve regresar a Alberto.
Viene solo. Abre. Entra. Las luces han vuelto a su intensidad natural.
Alberto respira abiertamente. Deja su sombrero junto a su abrigo. Después de lanzar una mirada a los muebles, acomoda los sillones como
al final del primer acto. Luego, apaga la luz del fondo. Queda la
luz de la lámpara de mesa. Se sienta en el sillón de la izquierda.
Consulta el reloj. Se estremece. Y luego, queda poco a poco inmóvil,
sin volver la cara, con una mirada fija y vacía, delante de sí, estreme-
ciéndose."

Alberto *(en voz baja, como para sí): ¿*Es usted, padre? ¿Es usted?
Obras, p. 406.

24. ". . . el fantasma de un Hipólito muerto por la cólera requerida a
los dioses. . . ."

25. ". . . 'furor' que ha de ahogar en el suicidio. . . ."

26. For Martínez' complete argument, see his "Esquema de un
año de literatura mexicana," *Letras de México*, IV, 13 (enero 1942),
13; reprinted as "La literatura mexicana en 1941" in his *Literatura
mexicana siglo XX*, vol. 1. Mexico, 1949, p. 113.

27. "Teresa tiene unos treinta y cinco años. Es alta y fuerte. Se
diría que bajo su piel de un color vegetal circula savia en vez de
sangre. El aire y la luz la turban y la hacen sentir más profundamente.
Se diría también que de todos los objetos que toca, que de todos
los seres que abraza, extrae, insensiblemente, algo que le enriquece.
Y se adivina que la oscuridad y la soledad completas, la empobrecerían
definitivamente." *Obras*, p. 257.

28. "Teresa es como la hiedra: vive de lo que toca, de lo que abraza.
Tu padre me lo decía con otras palabras: 'Siento que soy yo quien
da vida, calor y fuego a esta criatura.' Conozco a seres como Teresa,
y te confieso que no solo hay un placer inmenso en dejar que se
apoyen en nosotros sino también en el desfallecimiento que sigue a
esa transfusión de sangre, de savia, en que se resuelve para nosotros

su contacto. Basta que sientas una de sus manos apoyarse en la tuya o asirla, para sentir que se establece esa misteriosa transfusión." *Obras,* p. 273.

29. "Nuestras vidas están siempre en equilibrio inestable. El bien y el mal son las pesas de la balanza. Un día decidimos—o alguien decide por nosotros—no seguir haciendo el mal que hacíamos a una persona. Pero no por eso desaparece el mal. El mal sigue siendo el mismo, sólo que ahora se ejerce en otra dirección, recae en otra persona que en la mayoría de los casos es inocente." *Obras,* p. 274.

30. "Querer hacer el bien y solamente el bien equivaldría a salir a la calle un día de sol y pretender que nuestro cuerpo no haga sombra." *Obras,* p. 275.

31. "¡Estoy sola! ¡Estoy sola otra vez!" *Obras,* p. 270.

32. "La literatura mexicana en 1942," *Literatura mexicana siglo XX,* Mexico, 1949, 135.

33. "¡Ha sido un impulso muy humano y muy hermoso retirar de aquí ese retrato! ¡Pero ahora, Marta, que sabe usted lo que pienso, puede usted ponerlo otra vez en el sitio en que ha estado siempre . . . en el que estará siempre!" *Obras,* p. 320.

34. "Para que, desde el retrato, me vea salir . . . del mismo modo que el día en que llegué a esta casa lo quitó, para que no me viera entrar. . . ." *Obras,* p. 342.

35. ". . . con una mirada en que no habrá la menor sombra de piedad ni de triunfo sino una intensa y profunda comprensión." *Obras,* p. 320.

36. Here we have again an example of Villaurrutia's punning use of similar sounds. Literally translated, the title means "The Burning Error," but the same sound pattern also stands for "The Burning Iron." Here, this usage seems to have no direct bearing on the play, except to suggest—rather remotely—the scars which all concerned will forever bear, as though applied by a hot iron. It is not one of Villaurrutia's most felicitous examples of this custom.

37. This is a fairly common theme, and specific antecedents are difficult to determine. Two treatments which Villaurrutia is likely to have known are Benito Pérez Galdós' *El abuelo,* based on *King Lear,* and Dumas the Younger's *Le fils naturel.*

38. "Un clavo ardiendo," *Letras de México,* V, III (mayo 1945), 86.

39. "Una sonrisa en el rostro ceñudo del teatro mexicano." Quoted by Antonio Magaña Esquivel, *Sueño y realidad del teatro,* 138.

40. Beatriz: Parece ser que, al menos entre cierta clase social, en Guadalajara la psicopatología de la vida cotidiana es de una variedad y riqueza increíbles.

Carmen: Beatriz quiere decir que en Guadalajara abundan los adulterios, los divorcios, las fugas y los triángulos. *Obras,* p. 466.

41. Beatriz *(a Don Lucas):* Este compromiso es tan imprevisto. ¿No le parece? Sospecho que aquí hay un complejo sumergido. *Obras,* p. 474.

42. Beatriz: Carmen cree que ser soltera es una cualidad.
Virginia: Que va dejando de serlo a medida que pasa el tiempo. Carmen ha cultivado esta cualidad, hasta ahora, con mucho éxito; pero, por lo visto, ya le va cansando, ¿verdad, querida?
Carmen *(con firmeza):* Si me va cansando o no, es cuenta mía y solo mía. Nunca te he hecho notar que después de cansarte de ser soltera, te cansaste de ser casada y empiezas a dar muestras de fatiga ahora que estás divorciada.
Amparo: ¡El Maratón del cansancio! Toma asiento, Virginia. Debes de estar muy fatigada. *Obras,* pp. 464-465.

43. "No es preciso que digan nada. ¡Si ya sé lo que van a decir! . . . Vayan, vayan ustedes también. Yo iré después. Ahora, dejen solo un momento a este pobre, a este pobre Barba Azul." *Obras,* p. 511.

44. El Poeta: Buenas noches, doctor. *(Y luego con un estremecimiento casi imperceptible, en un tono que no puede dejar de ser de complicidad dolorosa, añade):* Por lo que toca a este asunto, yo *tampoco* le diré nada a mi esposa. *Obras,* p. 190.

45. Nora Badía, "Mañana es una palabra," *Nueva Generación,* I, 2 (feb. 1950), 5-9; Víctor Manuel Díez Barroso, *Siete Obras en un Acto,* México, 1935.

46. "Teatro y cinematografía: Convergencias y Divergencias," *Cuadernos Americanos,* XXXIII, 3 (mayo-junio 1947), 221-236.

47. ". . . una concentración sorprendente del espacio y del tiempo," *op. cit.,* p. 235.

48. "Pasión y verdad en el teatro de Villaurrutia," *Revista Iberoamericana,* XXVIII, 54 (julio-diciembre, 1962), 337-46.

49. *Semblanzas mexicanas,* 144.

50. *The Idea of a Theater,* Garden City, 1953, esp. pp. 31ff.

Chapter Four

1. "El teatro de Xavier Villaurrutia," *Cuadernos Americanos,* 1952, XI, 2, 288.

2. "¡Qué dulce el agua disolviendo sales!" "Arroyo."

3. Eras como el agua
un rostro movido, ¡ay!,
cortado
por el metal de los reflejos.

4. *Hispania,* XLIII, 2, May 1960, 205-78.

5. *Obras,* 208.

6. "Correlación y paralelismo en la poesía de Xavier Villaurrutia," *La Palabra y el Hombre,* 37 (enero-marzo 1966), 81-90.

7. See Dámaso Alonso and Carlos Bousoño, *Seis calas en la expresión literaria española,* 2nd ed., 1956.

8. "Con Xavier Villaurrutia," 79.

9. "El romanticismo y el sueño," *Romance,* año 1 (15 sept. 1940), 2.

10. ". . . en virtud de la ley de menor esfuerzo, todo lo romántico ha quedado peligrosamente reducido a designar, casi siempre, lo desordenado, lo espontáneo, cuando no el verbalismo o la elocuencia," *op. cit.,* p. 1.

11. "la inquietud y la angustia ante el misterio cósmico, la nostalgia de lo conocido, la zozobra ante lo desconocido y las oscilaciones del espíritu en los mundos de la vigilia y el sueño." "Prologo," *Laurel. Antología de la Poesía Moderna en Lengua Española,* eds. Villaurrutia, J. Gil Albert, Octavio Paz, and Emilio Prados (México, 1941), p. 9.

12. ". . . despertar del alma y . . . despertar al sueño. . . ." "El Romanticismo . . . ," p. 2.

13. ". . . toda época del pensamiento humano podría definirse, de manera profunda, por las relaciones que establece entre el sueño y la vigilia . . . ," *loc. cit.*

14. Bernardo Ortiz de Montellano *et al., Una botella al mar,* México, Edit. Rueca, 1946.

15. ". . . esa inteligencia permanentemente lúcida, inalterable por la pasión." *El trato con escritores,* la. serie, México, 1961, 133.

16. ". . . quizá existan en mi obra, más que influencia de algunos escritores, la de un pintor. En Chirico encontré muchas veces una clara afinidad." "Con Xavier Villaurrutia," 79.

17. "Teatro y Cinematografía: Convergencias y Divergencias," *Cuadernos Americanos,* XXXIII, 3 (mayo-junio 1947), 221-36.

18. Rilke, "Fourth Elegy," *Duino Elegies,* trans. by J. B. Leishman and Stephen Spender. New York, 1939, p. 45.

19. *Rainer Maria Rilke,* New York, 1941, p. 167.

20. Quoted by Guillermo de Torre, *La aventura y el orden,* Buenos Aires, 1948, p. 151.

21. *Rainer Maria Rilke: Masks and the Man,* Seattle, 1960, p. 65.

22. Frank Wood, *Rainer Maria Rilke: The Ring of Forms,* Minneapolis, 1958, p. 53.

23. *Op. cit.,* p. 183.

24. Wood, *op. cit.,* p. 182.

25. *Duino Elegies,* p. 87.

26. "La poesía de Xavier Villaurrutia," *Estaciones,* I, 4 (invierno 1956), 462.

27. Cocteau, *Five Plays,* New York, 1961, p. 2.

28. *Five Plays,* p. 215.

29. *Ibid.*, p. 29.

30. *Jean Cocteau*, New York, 1956, p. 80.

31. "La muerte en la poesía de Xavier Villaurrutia," *Cuadernos de Bellas Artes*, I, 5 dic. 1960.

32. *Obras*, p. xix.

33. Saisir:
    Saisir, saisir le soir, la pomme et la statue,
    saisir l'ombre et la mur et la bout de la rue
    Saisir le pied, le cou de la femme couchée
    et puis ouvrir les mains, combres d'oiseaux lâchés.
    Combien d'oiseaux perdus qui deviennent la rue,
    L'ombre, le mur, le soir, la pomme et la statue.
    Choix de poèmes, Paris, 7th ed., 1947, p. 89.

34. Nocturno de la estatua:
    Soñar, soñar la noche, la calle, la escalera
    y el grito de la estatua desdoblando la esquina.
    Correr hacia la estatua y encontrar sólo el grito,
    querer tocar el grito y sólo hallar el eco,
    querer asir el eco y encontrar sólo el muro
    y correr hacia el muro y tocar un espejo.

35. Jules Supervielle, *Inédits, oeuvres choisis* . . . , étude par Claude Roy. Paris, 1961, p. 18.

36. "Villaurrutia, poeta," *Hoy*, 724 (6 enero 1951), 38.

37. "La seul immortalité des morts est celle que leur accordent les fidélités des mortels . . . ,"*Inédits* . . . , 24.

38. *Jules Supervielle: A Modern Fabulist*, Oxford, 1960, p. 15.

39. *Ibid.*, p. 42.

40. "Poetas de América: Xavier Villaurrutia, Corazón y Profundidad," *América Española*, 42-43 (agosto-sept. 1941), 210-13.

41. Two basic sources are Octavio Paz, *The Labyrinth of Solitude*, trans. by Lysander Kemp, Grove Press, 1961, and the November 1948 issue of *México en el Arte*.

42. México-Buenos Aires, 2nd ed., 1949, p. 56.

43. México, 1940.

44. Lloro y me aflijo, cuando recuerdo
    que dejaremos las bellas flores,
    los bellos cantos:

Gocemos, cantemos: todos nos vamos
y nos perdemos. . . .

45. Porque no lo comprenden así mis amigos,
está doliente y se aira mi corazón:
no por segundo vez serán engendrados,
no por segunda vez serán hechos hijos,
y ya están a punto de salir de la tierra.

46. Tu corazón lo sabe: ¡una sola vez
hemos venido a vivir!

47. No hago más que sufrir, porque solo
en angustias vivimos.
Canto de orfandad.

48. Nunca en verdad cesará, nunca en verdad
se irá,
ni se me hará soportable la tristeza que
ahora expreso.
Canto en loor de los reyes.

49. Solo venimos a dormir, solo venimos
a soñar:
no es verdad, no es verdad que venimos
a vivir en la tierra.
Vida efímera.

50. Mariano Picón-Salas, *De la Conquista a la Independencia*,
México-Buenos Aires, 1944, p. 25.

51. *Op. cit.*, p. 32.

52. "La lírica nahuatl en la poesía moderna mexicana," *Revista
de la Universidad de México*, XIX, 5(enero 1965), 23-25.

53. *Vocabulario mexicano relativo a la muerte*, México, 1963, p. 5.

54. México, 13th ed., 1947, 216.

55. "Ese medio tono insistente, monótono, que pesa en nuestra
lírica y que hasta parece un molde escogido a priori. . . ." *Obras*, p. 820.

56. "Las características de la poesía mexicana de este medio siglo
son las mismas características del mexicano selecto que es, por esencia,
reflexivo, introvertido, discreto e intimista. Por ello, la poesía mexicana
tiene ese suave y melodioso medio tono." "Y ahora hablemos de la
poesía mexicana," *Hoy*, 723, 30 dic. 1950, 27.

57. *Obras*, p. 765.

58. ". . . delicado equilibrio del pensamiento con la forma, de la idea
y de la frase, de la sustancia y del perfil," 4.

59. *Imagen de la poesía mexicana contemporánea*, México, 1959, p. 17.

60. *El laberinto de la soledad*, México, 2nd ed., 1959, p. 56.

Chapter Five

1. "Carta a un poeta," *Hoy*, 151 (13 enero 1940), 41.

2. "Villaurrutia, poeta," *Hoy*, 724 (6 enero 1951).

3. *El trato con escritores*, Mexico, 1964, 2a serie, 60.

4. "El teatro y la amistad en Xavier Vlliaurrutia," *Cuadernos de Bellas Artes*, I, 5 dic. 1960, 11.

5. *Op. cit.*, p. 13.

6. *Teatro messicano del '900*, p. 36.

7. Rodolfo Usigli, "Estética de la muerte," *El Hijo Pródigo* (15 julio 1946), 29-31.

8. *Obras*, p. xxx.

Selected Bibliography

Complete or Selected Works:

Poesía y teatro completos. Prologue by Alí Chumacero. Mexico, Fondo de Cultura Económica, 1953.

Obras. Prologue by Alí Chumacero. Recopilation of texts by Miguel Capistrán, Alí Chumacero and Luis Mario Schneider. Bibliography by Luis Mario Schneider. Mexico, Fondo de Cultura Económica, 1966, 2nd edition, augmented.

Poetry:

Reflejos. Mexico, Edit. Cultura, 1926.
Dos nocturnos. Mexico, Barandal, 1931.
Nocturnos. Mexico, Fábula, 1931.
Nocturno de los Angeles. Mexico, Hipocampo, 1936.
Nocturno mar. Mexico, Hipocampo, 1937.
Nostalgia de la muerte. Buenos Aires, Sur, 1938; Mexico, Mictlán, 1946, 2nd edition.
Décima muerte y otros poemas no coleccionados. Mexico, Nueva Voz, 1941.
Canto a la Primavera y otros poemas. Mexico, Stylo, 1948.

Plays:

Parece mentira. Mexico, Mundial, 1934.
¿En qué piensas? Mexico, Letras de México, 1938.
Sea Ud. breve. Mexico, Cuadernos de México Nuevo, 1938.
Autos profanos. Mexico, Letras de México, 1941.
La hiedra. Mexico, Nueva Cultura, 1941.
La mujer legítima. Mexico, Loera y Chávez, 1943.
Invitación a la muerte. Mexico, Letras de México, 1944; 2nd edition, Teatro Mexicano Contemporáneo, 1948.
El yerro candente. Mexico, Letras de México, 1945.
El pobre Barba Azul. Mexico, Teatro Mexicano Contemporáneo, 1948.
La tragedia de las equivocaciones. México Gráficos Guanajuato, 1950.
El solterón. Mexico, Colección Teatro Mexicano, 1954.

Fiction:

Dama de Corazones. Mexico, Ulises, 1928.

SECONDARY SOURCES

Books:

BELLINI, GIUSEPPE. *Teatro messicano del '900.* Milano, Instituto Editoriale Cisalpino, 1959. Includes an excellent chapter on Villaurrutia.

DAUSTER, FRANK. *Ensayos sobre poesía mexicana.* Mexico, Edics. De Andrea, 1963. A study of the generation of the "Contemporáneos" and of the poetry of the leading figures of the movement.

FORSTER, MERLIN. *Los Contemporáneos.* Mexico, Edics. De Andrea, 1964. An analysis of the origins of the generation of the Contemporáneos and their work during the early years of the movement.

LEIVA, RAUL. *Imagen de la poesía mexicana contemporánea.* Mexico, Imprenta Universitaria, 1959. Leiva's strong political bias does not prevent him from presenting a strong analysis of Villaurrutia's major themes and his standing among his generation.

MAGANA ESQUIVEL, ANTONIO. *Imagen del teatro.* Mexico, Letras de México, 1940.

————. *Sueño y realidad del teatro.* Mexico, Instituto Nacional de Bellas Artes, 1949.

————. *Medio siglo de teatro mexicano.* Mexico, Instituto Nacional de Bellas Artes, 1964. Magaña Esquivel's works are the best introduction to modern Mexican theater, and essential reading for an understanding of the background of Villaurrutia's work.

REYES NEVAREZ, SALVADOR. *El amor y la amistad en el mexicano.* Mexico, n.p., 1952. Includes a perceptive essay on the role of love in Villaurrutia's poetry.

XIRAU, RAMON. *Tres poetas de la soledad.* Mexico, Antigua Librería Robredo, 1966. "Presencia de una ausencia," devoted to Villaurrutia's poetry, is one of the best studies to date.

Articles:

BELLINI, GIUSEPPE. "La poesia de Xavier Villaurrutia." *Literatture Moderne,* X (gennaio-febbraio, 1960), 20-27. A careful analysis of the poetry.

BRUSHWOOD, JOHN S. "Contemporáneos and the Limits of Art." *Romance Notes,* V (1964), 2, 1-5. Excellent discussion of the attack on the Contemporáneos.

FORSTER, MERLIN H. "The 'Contemporaneos:' A major group in Mexican vanguardism." *Texas Studies in Language and Literature*, III, 4 (Winter, 1962), 425-38. An excellent brief survey of the period of the review, *Contemporáneos*.

MARTINEZ, JOSE LUIS. "Con Xavier Villaurrutia." *Tierra Nueva*, I, 2 (marzo-abril, 1940), 74-81. The poet's answers to Martínez' interview provide the best source for Villaurrutia's poetics.

NANDINO, ELIAS. "La poesía de Xavier Villaurrutia." *Estaciones*, I, 4 (invierno, 1956), 460-68. Villaurrutia's physician and close friend provides a number of insights and critical background information.

RODRIGUEZ CHICHARRO, CESAR. "Disemia y paronomasia en la poesía de Xavier Villaurrutia." *La Palabra y el Hombre*, abril-junio, 1964, 249-60.

————. "Correlación y paralelismo en la poesía de Xavier Villaurrutia." *La Palabra y El Hombre*, 37 (enero-marzo, 1966), 81-90. Careful technical analyses of some of Villaurrutia's key poetic procedures.

SHAW, DONALD. "Pasión y verdad en el teatro de Villaurrutia." *Revista Iberoamericana*, XXVIII, 54 (julio-dic., 1962), 337-46. An illuminating study of the search for individual truth as the basic theme of Villaurrutia's plays.

CUADERNOS DE BELLAS ARTES, I, 5 (diciembre, 1960). Includes several articles on Villaurrutia.

REVISTA DE BELLAS ARTES, 7 (enero-febrero, 1966). Contains important unpublished material.

Index